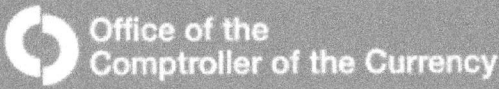
Office of the
Comptroller of the Currency

Semiannual Risk Perspective

From the National Risk Committee

Office of the Comptroller of the Currency
Washington, D.C.

Spring 2014

Table of Contents

About This Report

The Office of the Comptroller of the Currency (OCC) charters, regulates, and supervises national banks and federal savings associations[1] (collectively, banks) and supervises the federal branches and agencies of foreign banks. The OCC supervises these banks to ensure they operate in a safe and sound manner and comply with applicable laws and regulations, including those requiring fair treatment of consumers and fair access to credit and financial products.

The OCC's National Risk Committee (NRC) monitors the condition of the federal banking system and emerging threats to the system's safety and soundness. NRC members include senior agency officials who supervise banks of all sizes, as well as officials from the law, policy, accounting, and economics departments. The NRC meets quarterly and issues guidance to examiners that provides perspective on industry trends and highlights issues requiring attention.

The OCC's *Semiannual Risk Perspective* addresses key issues facing banks. The OCC publishes the report twice a year, drawing upon midyear and year-end data. The spring 2014 report reflects data as of December 31, 2013.

Banks face risks and opportunities. As a report discussing risks, the *Semiannual Risk Perspective* focuses on issues that pose threats to the safety and soundness of banks rather than opportunities that banks may encounter at the same time. Other available sources assess opportunities and discuss the upside potential of those opportunities. This report presents data in five main areas: the operating environment; the condition and performance of the banking system; key risk issues; elevated risk metrics; and regulatory actions.

The OCC welcomes feedback on this report by e-mail: NRCReport@occ.treas.gov.

---

[1] The Dodd–Frank Wall Street Reform and Consumer Protection Act of 2010 (Dodd–Frank Act) transferred supervision of federal savings associations to the OCC on July 21, 2011.

Executive Summary

The financial performance of federally chartered institutions improved in 2013. The federal banking system set a new record level of net income in 2013, but this took seven years and $1.5 trillion (or 20 percent) growth in assets to achieve, highlighting the slow pace of the recovery from the recent financial crisis. This new nominal record was only $5 billion (5 percent) higher than the previous record set before the financial crisis in 2006. Return on assets and return on equity remain below pre-recession peaks. Overall, the federal banking system returned almost 10 percent on equity, but small banks continue to lag behind larger ones. Revenue declined modestly as lower net interest income more than offset modestly higher noninterest income. Sluggish loan growth and prolonged low interest rates continue to weigh on net interest margins (NIM). The improvement in earnings still comes largely from lower noninterest and provision expenses instead of organic growth.

Economic fundamentals showed improvement as households deleveraged, household wealth increased, and credit availability improved. With consumers feeling more confident, they are spending more. Businesses overall are profitable, and industrial production has been rising. Moreover, fiscal drag from higher taxes and lower government spending is fading. On the negative side, unemployment continues to weigh on economic growth as payrolls are just now returning to their pre-recession peak, and many of the long-term unemployed may permanently leave the labor force.

Traditional credit risk metrics improved significantly in 2013. The level of problem assets declined as economic conditions improved. The level of nonperforming assets and net charge-offs declined substantially and are now back near or below pre-recession levels. Allowance for loan and lease losses (ALLL) releases were a common practice for many banks in 2013, driven by the improvement in loan quality and moderate portfolio growth. Median loan growth remains below average. Commercial loan growth, however, has been stronger, particularly for larger banks, but the pace of loan growth varies widely at small banks.

The OCC sees signs that credit risk is now building after a period of improving credit quality and problem loan clean-up. Examiners have observed erosion in the underwriting standards for syndicated leveraged loans, as well as loosening of standards and increased layering of risk in the indirect auto market. Recent examinations of commercial loan portfolios have identified an increase in policy and underwriting exceptions, including some examples of risk layering (e.g., increasing collateral advance rates, waiving or loosening of guarantees, and more liberal repayment terms such as extended periods of interest-only payments). A recent horizontal review of midsize and community bank asset-based lending (ABL) found evidence of gradually loosening credit policies in response to competitive pressures. Further, bankers are speaking out increasingly regarding their concern with competitive pressures. Given these trends, the OCC will increase its attention on underwriting standards and encourage banks to diligently assess their credit risk appetite in this stage of the credit cycle.

The industry continues to face significant challenges. The limited ability to increase revenue and operating profit (income before provision expense) remains a key challenge. Low interest rates, slow total loan growth, and inconsistent fee income patterns still hinder revenue gains, while lower loan-loss provision expense is a key support to increased profits. Longer-term interest rates moved higher in 2013 while monetary policy continues to keep short-term rates at or near historical lows. Concerns over sovereign debt, weak economic and credit growth, and fiscal and monetary policy uncertainty in Europe, the United States, Japan, and emerging markets continue to limit gains in business and consumer confidence, weighing on the pace of global economic growth.

Key Risk Themes

Strategic risk remains high for many banks as management teams search for sustainable ways to generate target rates of return.

- Many banks continue to reevaluate their business models, deployment of capital, and risk appetites given the challenging operating environment. Some banks are taking on additional risks by expanding into new, less familiar, or higher-risk products.
- Some banks are lowering overhead expenses, often by reductions in control functions, exiting less profitable businesses, closing offices, and outsourcing critical control functions to third parties, in some instances without appropriate levels of due diligence.[2]
- Banks continue to face competitive pressure from nonbank firms seeking to expand into traditional banking activities.
- Management succession planning and retaining key experienced personnel is a growing issue for many banks.

Banks' boards of directors and senior managers should ensure that strategic planning and product approval processes appropriately consider the requisite expertise, management information systems (MIS) and risk controls for the banks' business lines and activities.[3] Banks also should incorporate management succession and retention of key personnel into their strategic planning process.

Competitive pressures, the need for revenue growth, the ongoing low interest rate environment, and compliance challenges continue to complicate bank risk management.

- Competition is resulting in eased underwriting across a variety of products. Weakening standards are particularly evident in indirect auto and leveraged lending; however, some easing in underwriting and increased risk layering are also occurring in other types of commercial loans. While not widespread, some examiners note multiple policy and underwriting exceptions on individual credit decisions. The OCC's "Survey of Credit Underwriting Practices" and the Federal Reserve Board's "Senior Loan Officer Opinion Survey on Bank Lending Practices" underscore these findings.
- ALLL releases continue despite the risk building in many loan portfolios. Given these trends, ongoing ALLL releases are not a sustainable source of earnings.
- The increase in long-term interest rates in 2013 underscores the need to understand and quantify banks' vulnerability to rising interest rates. The prolonged low interest rate environment continues to lay the foundation for future vulnerability. Some banks have reached for yield to boost interest income with decreasing regard for interest rate or credit risk. Banks that extend asset maturities to pick up yield, especially if relying on the stability of non-maturity deposit funding in a rising rate environment, could face significant earnings pressure and potential capital erosion depending on the severity and timing of interest rate moves.
- Financial asset prices have experienced very low volatility for an extended period. As a result, measures of price risk, such as value-at-risk (VaR), are at very low levels. The reduced willingness

---

[2] OCC Bulletin 2013-29, "Third-Party Relationships: Risk Management Guidance," provides guidance to banks for assessing and managing risks associated with third-party relationships.

[3] OCC Bulletin 2004-20, "Risk Management of New, Expanded, or Modified Bank Products and Services," provides guidance on processes to prudently manage the risks associated with new, expanded, or modified bank products and services.

of dealers to hold securities in inventory, due to capital and other concerns such as a change in monetary policy, could contribute to greater price swings going forward and increased price risk.

- Bank Secrecy Act (BSA) and anti–money laundering (AML) risks remain prevalent given changing methods of money laundering and growth in the volume and sophistication of electronic banking fraud. BSA/AML risk has increased among community banks during 2012–2013, resulting from increases in the number of higher-risk, cash-intensive customers and internationally oriented transactions. In addition, BSA programs at some banks have failed to evolve or incorporate appropriate controls into new products and services. A lack of resources and expertise devoted to BSA/AML risk management in some banks often compounds these issues.

Banks' boards of directors and senior managers need to monitor elevated policy exceptions to established underwriting standards and be alert to the product terms that layer on additional risks. ALLL processes should be reviewed to determine whether additional qualitative adjustments are needed to reflect the increased risk in loan portfolios. Banks with significant concentrations in longer-term assets should assess their vulnerability to a sudden rise in interest rates. Banks also need to understand and quantify how their non-maturity depositors will react to rising rates and ensure that model assumptions correlate. Compliance programs should keep pace with the volume and complexity of regulatory changes and changes in bank customers and transactions.

Operational risk remains high because of the volume and velocity of change to business models and operations as well as continuing cyber-threats.

- The volume and velocity of change in technology systems and business processes continue to increase. Banks are challenged to manage the change process, ensure adequate resources and process capacity, and maintain quality and controls. Business lines and functional areas within banks must perform thorough risk and control self-assessments, analyze operational events, and identify, assess, monitor, and mitigate emerging risks. Risk management is balancing resource constraints, retention of key talent, and overall capability to monitor the breadth of change.
- Banks continue to be attractive targets of coordinated and sophisticated cyber-attacks. Recurring security breaches at retail merchants highlight the interdependencies in today's payment systems. Additionally, there is concern that cyber-criminals will transition from disruptive attacks to attacks that are intended to cause destruction and corruption. These threats require heightened awareness and appropriate resources to identify and mitigate the evolving risks. Federal banking supervisors issued statements on three cyber-threats and vulnerabilities in April 2014.[4]
- The number, nature, and complexity of both foreign and domestic third-party relationships continue to expand, resulting in increased system and process interconnectedness and additional vulnerability to cyber-threats.
- As banks seek new lines of business, some are bundling products and services or assuming new roles as agents between consumers and merchants that increase cross-channel payment, operational, and compliance risks.

---

[4] OCC Bulletin 2014-13, "Cyber Attacks on Financial Institutions' Automated Teller Machine and Card Authorization Systems: Joint Statement," notifies banks of a large-dollar-value automated teller machine cash-out fraud characterized as "Unlimited Operations" by the U.S. Secret Service and provides guidance on supervisory expectations to mitigate this threat. OCC Bulletin 2014-14, "Distributed Denial-of-Service Cyber Attacks, Risk Mitigation, and Additional Resources: Joint Statement," notifies banks of the risks associated with the continued distributed denial-of-service attacks and the steps that institutions are expected to take to address these attacks. OCC Bulletin 2014-17, "Information Security Vulnerability in OpenSSL Encryption Tool (Heartbleed): Joint Statement," notifies banks of a material security vulnerability in OpenSSL, a widely used encryption tool. The alert outlines the risks associated with this vulnerability (also known as Heartbleed) and the risk mitigation steps that financial institutions are expected to take to address those risks.

- The Dodd–Frank Act and international regulations to promote the use of central counterparties (CCP) for clearing and settlement, while reducing counterparty risks among individual derivatives, are resulting in rapid growth in foreign CCP memberships with potential risk exposures to various legal and political environments. The increased use of CCPs means that credit risk that was more widely distributed on a bilateral basis has become more concentrated in CCPs.

Bankers should maintain heightened awareness and appropriate resources to identify and mitigate cyber-threats and vulnerabilities. Bankers should also ensure that risk management of third-party relationships is commensurate with the breadth, complexity, and criticality of these arrangements as outlined in OCC Bulletin 2013-29.

OCC Risk Perspective: Outlook by OCC Business Line

Large Banks

Core profitability at OCC-supervised large banks is negatively affected by anemic spread income and significantly lower fee income from mortgage banking activities. Large litigation expenses are adversely affecting aggregate net income, though ALLL releases and cost savings offset some of the earnings pressure. Capital, asset quality, and liquidity continue to improve.

Key risk issues facing large banks include

- a high level of operational risk across a spectrum of activities.
- increasing volume and sophistication of cyber-threats.
- compliance and BSA/AML risks.
- third-party arrangements that introduce concentration risk.
- erosion of underwriting standards because of competitive pressures, particularly in indirect auto and leveraged lending.

The outlook for large banks includes

- modest loan growth throughout 2014.
- slower NIM contraction. Cyclical expansion is possible in 2015 and beyond, after the impact of a future rise in short-term rates becomes evident.
- slowing ALLL releases. The earnings benefit from ALLL releases has started to abate and is expected to continue dissipating in 2014.

Community and Midsize Banks

The overall financial condition of community and midsize banks supervised by the OCC continues to improve, as reflected by positive trends in asset quality indicators. The earnings outlook for this segment of the banking industry, however, is less uniform. While earnings overall are improving because of loan growth, expanding business lines, and reduced provision and other real estate owned expenses, pressures persist at many small banks due to weak loan demand and declining investment yields.

Key risk issues facing community and midsize banks include

- higher strategic risk as banks adapt their business models to respond to sluggish economic growth,

the low interest rate environment, and competitive pressures.
- planning for management succession and retention of key staff.
- erosion of underwriting standards.
- expansion into loan products that require specialized risk management processes and skills.
- increased exposure to interest rate risk (IRR) at some banks related to concentrations of agency-issued mortgage-backed securities (MBS) and unsupported non-maturity deposit assumptions.
- appropriate oversight of third parties that perform operational and business functions.
- increasing volume and sophistication of cyber-threats.
- increasing BSA/AML risk due to higher-risk services and customer relationships, particularly in community banks.

The outlook for community and midsize banks includes

- modest loan growth and stabilizing NIM, flat to lower provision expense because of improvement in credit metrics, and stronger capital ratios.
- suppressed mortgage-banking revenue because of declining refinance activity and lower gain-on-sale margins.
- continued search for higher-yielding assets and profitable strategic business niches.
- expansion into new products and services to meet rate-of-return objectives.

OCC Supervisory Priorities for the Next 12 Months

The OCC's supervision and policy priorities are based on key risks. Key priorities are summarized below.

Large Bank Supervision

The OCC will execute supervisory strategies for each large bank that prioritize risks, achieve supervisory objectives, and effectively use OCC resources. Heightened supervisory attention will focus on:

- **Governance and oversight:** OCC supervisory staff will focus on progress toward meeting the OCC's heightened expectations for corporate governance and oversight in the 19 largest banks. These expectations include board willingness to provide credible challenge, talent management, and compensation processes; defining and communicating risk appetite across the company; development and maintenance of strong audit and independent risk management functions; and board responsibility to preserve the sanctity of the charter.
- **Operational risk:** Lapses in controls, operational processes, oversight, and the resulting effects across a bank's activities highlight the interconnectedness of risks and the importance of managing those risks in an integrated fashion throughout the entire bank. OCC supervisory staff will focus on bank risk management, including bank preparedness for assessing and continuously adjusting controls for the evolving cyber-threat environment.
- **Follow-up examination work on enforcement actions:** OCC supervisory staff will continue to focus on assessing the corrective actions taken to address articles in the foreclosure consent orders, including strengthening operational processes and implementing any necessary upgrades to systems and processes to meet enhanced mortgage-servicing requirements. OCC supervisory staff will also focus on performing timely follow-up of matters requiring attention (MRA) and enforcement actions related to BSA and the Unfair or Deceptive or Abusive Acts or Practices - Credit Practices Rule.

- **Credit underwriting:** OCC supervisory staff will review commercial and retail credit underwriting practices, especially for indirect auto and leveraged loans. Completion of the Shared National Credit horizontal is a particular focus in light of higher growth in commercial lending.
- **Compliance:** OCC supervisory staff will coordinate with the Consumer Financial Protection Bureau (CFPB) to determine compliance with consumer laws, regulations, and guidance. OCC supervisory staff will continue to assess compliance with the Flood Disaster Protection Act of 1973 and the Servicemembers Civil Relief Act of 2003, and focus on the adequacy of enterprise-wide compliance risk management, including BSA/AML programs, in response to evolving money-laundering schemes and the rapid pace of technological change. OCC staff will also assess banks' effectiveness in identifying and responding to applicable risks posed by new products and services and loosening underwriting.
- **New regulatory requirements:** OCC supervisory staff will develop and implement plans for assessing banks' compliance with new regulatory requirements, including those related to capital, liquidity, trading activities, residential mortgages, and risk retention.
- **Fair access:** OCC supervisory staff will continue to encourage banks to meet the needs of creditworthy borrowers and monitor their compliance with the Community Reinvestment Act (CRA), fair lending, and other consumer protection laws.

Community and Midsize Bank Supervision

The OCC will execute supervisory strategies for midsize and community banks that prioritize risks, achieve supervisory objectives, and effectively use OCC resources. Heightened supervisory attention will focus on:

- **Strategic planning:** OCC supervisory staff will focus on the adequacy of strategic, capital, and succession planning processes in light of assumed risks and planned initiatives, assessing whether appropriate risk management processes are established and followed.
- **Corporate governance:** OCC supervisory staff will reinforce the importance of sound corporate governance appropriately calibrated to the size and complexity of the individual bank.
- **Stress testing:** OCC supervisory staff will review the appropriateness of Dodd–Frank Act stress tests required and prepared by banks with more than $10 billion in assets.
- **Operational risk:** OCC supervisory staff will assess the operational risk from banks' contemplated changes to business models and responses to strategic opportunities, such as the introduction of new or revised business products, processes, or delivery channels. Examiners will focus on all phases of risk management including planning, due diligence, internal controls, reporting, contract negotiations, and ongoing monitoring. Robust preparation and contingency planning for operational or technology disruptions, as well as for natural disasters, remain essential.
- **Cyber-threats:** OCC supervisory staff will review programs for assessing the evolving threat environment and continuously adjusting controls, as well as for robust vulnerability assessments and timely correction, access management, and incident response programs.
- **Loan underwriting:** OCC supervisory staff will evaluate the underwriting practices for new or renewed loans in banks' indirect auto, ABL, middle market, commercial and industrial (C&I), commercial real estate (CRE), and energy portfolios for slippage in structure and terms.
- **IRR:** OCC supervisory staff will focus on IRR measurement processes to ensure that management properly assesses a bank's vulnerability to changes in interest rates and, as appropriate, implements measurement tools to monitor and control this risk. A bank's ability to accurately identify and quantify IRR in both assets and liabilities (e.g., investment securities and non-maturity deposits) under varying model scenarios will be a key focal point. Examiners will also monitor portfolio composition for changes in risk appetite.

- **Compliance:** OCC supervisory staff will assess effectiveness in complying with consumer laws, regulations, and guidance. Staff reviews will include applicable compliance, legal, and reputation risks posed by new products and services and emerging technologies, in particular, those that introduce higher compliance or reputation risk. Examiners will focus on the adequacy of BSA/AML programs to keep pace with rapidly evolving money-laundering schemes, as well as with new products, services, and customers.
- **Fair access:** OCC supervisory staff will continue to encourage banks to meet the needs of creditworthy borrowers. OCC staff also will continue to monitor banks' compliance with the CRA, fair lending, and other consumer protection laws.

Supervisory Policies and Processes

The OCC will continue implementing its internal strategic initiatives to improve the effectiveness and efficiency of bank supervision activities. Priorities include:

- **Peer review findings:** OCC managers and staff will develop and implement work plans to address the findings and recommendations of the international peer review team.[5]
- **Supervisory analytics:** OCC staff will work collaboratively to enhance analytical tools for examiners and MIS on bank performance. This will include benchmarks and performance dashboards, and improved tracking and reporting of MRAs and other enforcement actions.
- **Risk assessment:** The OCC will improve its ability to anticipate and address emerging risks by working effectively with the NRC, the Financial Stability Oversight Council, the Office of Financial Research, the Federal Reserve, the Federal Deposit Insurance Corporation, and the CFPB to identify systemic risk and related metrics.
- **Collaboration:** OCC managers and staff will stress collaborative efforts across the OCC and with other regulators to enhance the effectiveness and efficiency of all supervisory activities.
- **Technical assistance:** OCC examiners and subject matter experts will identify opportunities to supplement our supervisory activities with technical assistance, resource materials, comparative data, and tools that provide added benefit to community and midsize banks.
- **Industry outreach:** OCC managers and staff will conduct outreach sessions with the industry and other appropriate parties to present OCC perspectives on emerging issues, explain new policies and regulations, clarify supervisory expectations, and provide bankers the opportunity to discuss their concerns with regulators and peers.

---

[5] See OCC news release 2014-75, "OCC Announces Actions to Respond to International Peer Review Recommendations."

Part I: Operating Environment

U.S. economic fundamentals are improving. Households have deleveraged, household wealth has increased, and credit has become more available. Increased wealth has improved consumers' confidence and drawn them back to auto showrooms and shopping malls. Increased wealth has also contributed to the recovery in house prices and sales. Businesses overall are profitable and fiscal drag from higher taxes and lower government spending is fading. Nevertheless, payrolls only now are returning to their pre-recession peak, and many of the long-term unemployed may be permanently affected. The economy will continue to face challenges in 2014 from slack in the labor market and other sectors of the economy, and from slow growth abroad.

U.S. Economic Growth Still Constraining Labor Market Improvement

Real gross domestic product (GDP) increased 2.5 percent in the fourth quarter of 2013 from the fourth quarter of 2012 (see figure 1). That pace of growth equaled the 25-year average. The unemployment rate continues to decline, partly because of the decline in the labor force. The consensus of private sector forecasters is for economic growth to improve but remain restrained because of ongoing sluggish growth in Europe, the potential for an abrupt slowdown in emerging markets, and uncertainty regarding the U.S. fiscal situation. The consensus estimate is that unemployment will continue to decline but will remain above its 25-year average of 6 percent through the end of 2014.

Figure 1: GDP and Unemployment Trends

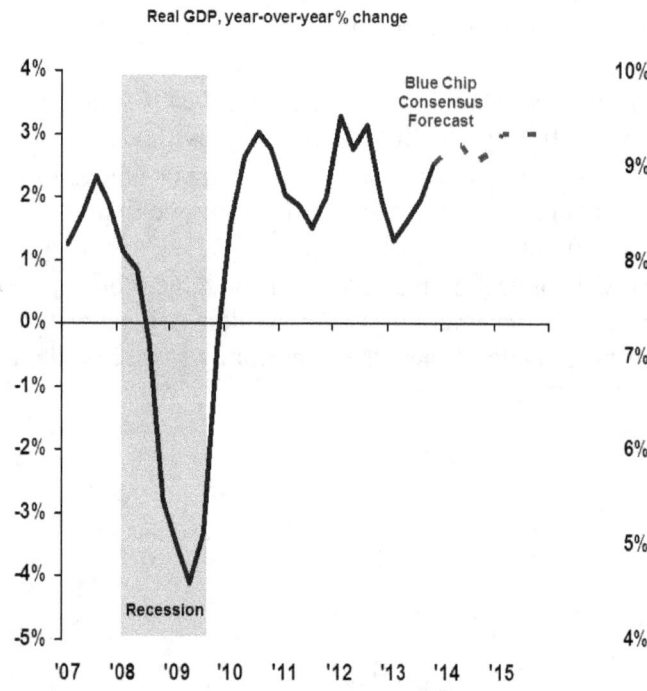

Sources: BEA, BLS/Haver Analytics, Blue Chip Indicators (March 2014)

Treasury Yields Remain Historically Low

Treasury yields have been at, or near, historical lows for the past several years. The slope of the yield curve steepened in 2013, in advance of the action by the Federal Reserve to "taper" bond purchases. The spread between 2-year and 10-year yields remains below its peak but has increased sharply to more than twice the historical median (see figure 2). An upward-sloping yield curve typically signals market expectations of an eventual increase in short-term interest rates in response to swifter economic growth and inflation. Banks would benefit from stronger growth, but the prolonged period of historically low interest rates, combined with limited loan demand, has led many banks to increase the size of their investment portfolios. Consequently, bank investment portfolios could develop concentrations of long-duration assets with fixed yields at historical lows. The historically low level of interest rates generally suggests that rates are likely to move sharply higher in response to any unexpected positive economic or higher inflation information. The most obvious negative effect of higher rates for banks is a further decline in the value of investment securities, including many mortgage-related securities. Another concern, however, is an increased debt service burden for borrowers. This risk is particularly acute for some marginal borrowers weakened during the recession who are now only meeting their debt obligations because of the current low rate climate.

Figure 2: Spread Between 2-Year and 10-Year U.S. Treasury Notes

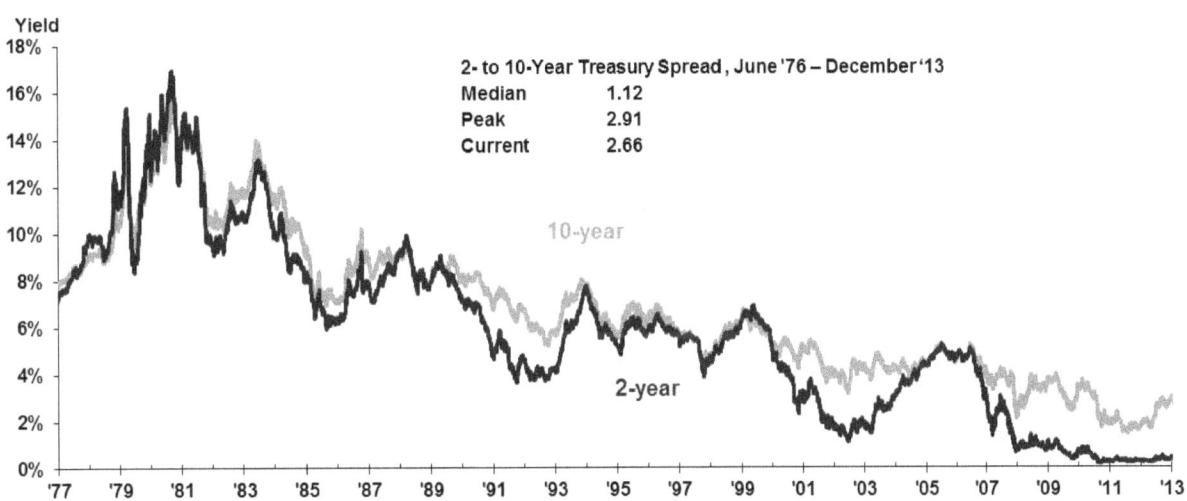

Source: Federal Reserve Board
Note: Treasury yield curve estimates, coupon equivalent par-yields. Data as of December 31, 2013.

Housing Metrics Continue to Improve

The housing market improved in 2013, as increased investor demand helped to significantly reduce the inventory of foreclosed and distressed homes, putting upward pressure on home prices. While still 21 percent below 2006 peak levels, Standard & Poor's Case-Shiller repeat-sales data show home prices up 11 percent year-over-year in 2013 (see figure 3). Nationally, mortgage performance improved for the fifth consecutive quarter, as delinquency rates and foreclosures continue to show improvement. The percentage of mortgages that are seriously delinquent declined to 3.5 percent from 4.4 percent a year earlier (see table 1). The percentage of foreclosures in process declined 37 percent from 3.3 percent of loans outstanding in the fourth quarter of 2012 to 2.1 percent in the fourth quarter of 2013. Most remaining distressed housing inventory (and thus future potential foreclosure risk) is increasingly concentrated in states with judicial foreclosure requirements.

Figure 3: S&P/Case-Shiller U.S. National Home Price Index

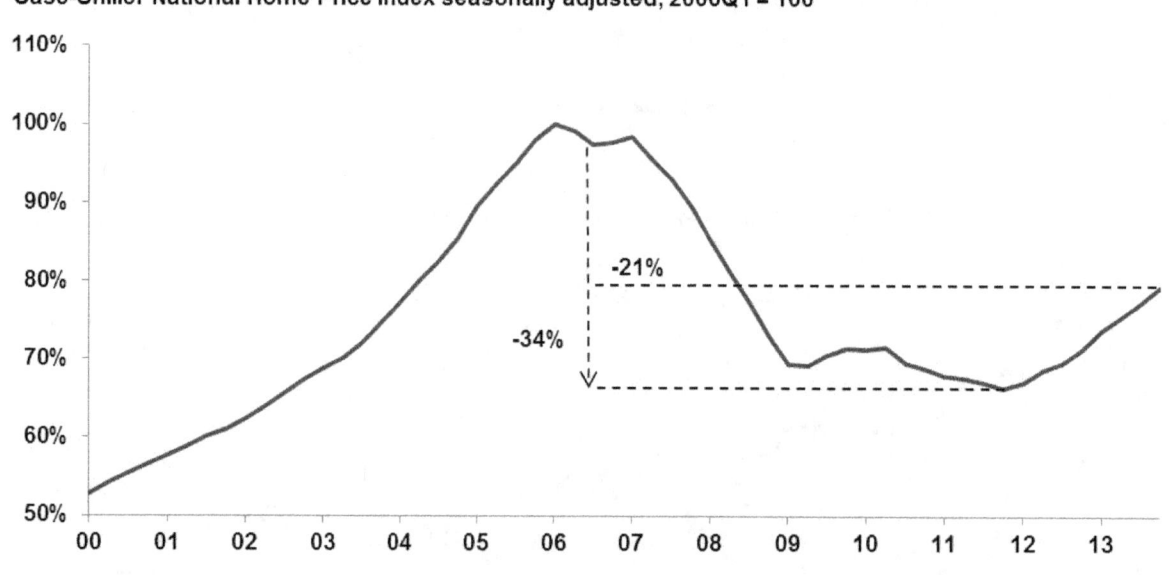

Case-Shiller National Home Price Index seasonally adjusted, 2006Q1 = 100

Source: Standard & Poor's

Table 1: Mortgage Portfolio Performance

	Percentage of Mortgages in the Portfolio						
	12/31/12	3/31/13	6/30/13	9/30/13	12/31/13	1Q %Change	1Y %Change
Current and Performing	89.4%	90.2%	90.6%	91.4%	91.8%	0.4%	2.7%
30–59 Days Delinquent	2.9%	2.6%	2.9%	2.6%	2.6%	-0.8%	-8.7%
The Following Three Categories Are Classified as Seriously Delinquent							
60–89 Days Delinquent	1.1%	0.9%	0.9%	0.9%	1.0%	1.9%	-10.8%
90 or More Days Delinquent	2.3%	2.1%	1.9%	1.8%	1.7%	-4.1%	-25.5%
Bankruptcy 30 or More Days Delinquent	1.0%	1.0%	1.0%	0.9%	0.8%	-7.9%	-20.2%
Subtotal for Seriously Delinquent	**4.4%**	**4.0%**	**3.8%**	**3.6%**	**3.5%**	**-3.5%**	**-20.7%**
Foreclosures in Process	3.3%	3.2%	2.8%	2.4%	2.1%	-10.9%	-37.0%

Source: *OCC Mortgage Metrics Report* for the Fourth Quarter of 2013.

Commercial Real Estate Vacancy Recovery Uneven Across Property Types

The CRE vacancy recovery under way since 2010 has been uneven across property types (see figure 4). Apartment vacancies returned to pre-recession levels before other property types, largely because the decline in homeownership increased apartment demand. Accordingly, apartment net operating incomes (NOI) are already above their previous peak and are expected to grow as rents increase further. Because of a significant increase in apartment construction, vacancy rates are rising in some markets, slowing the pace of growth in rental rates.

Office and retail vacancies continue to decline, although they remain higher than before the recession, as the trends of companies using less square footage per office worker, and consumers increasing online shopping, have reduced the demand for space. The warehouse recovery has recently accelerated because of online retailers opening more distribution centers while warehouse construction remains limited. For these three major nonresidential property types, however, average rents are still 5 percent to 12 percent below their previous peaks. Consequently, NOIs are near cyclical lows; also, many in-place leases continue to renew at lower rents.

Given expectations for an average pace of economic growth, most forecasts call for continued slow improvement in CRE market fundamentals. Property prices remain below peak for all property types at the national level, but the apartment sector outperforms other property types because of superior fundamentals. Low interest rates and stronger fundamentals have allowed CRE prices to begin to recover, but forecasters expect minimal improvement in commercial property values over the next two years since higher interest rates will partially offset the impact from strengthening fundamentals.

Figure 4: CRE Vacancy Rates

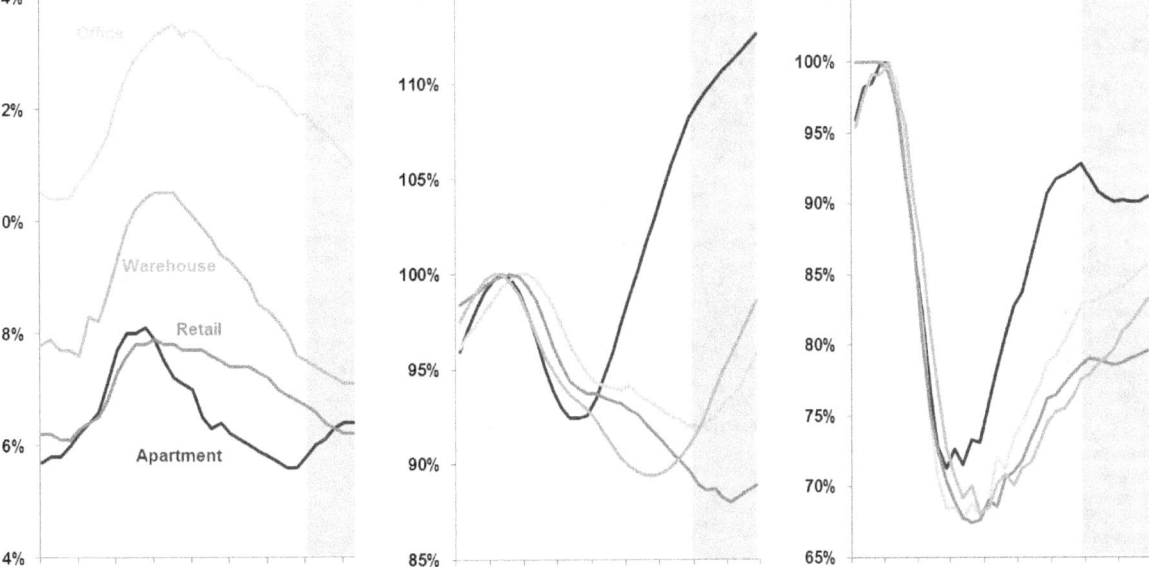

Source: Property & Portfolio Research; fourth quarter 2013 baseline PPR forecast

Part II: Condition and Performance of Banks

A. Profitability and Revenue: Improving Slowly

Profitability Increasing

Net income for 2013 set a new nominal record, increasing 12 percent from the prior year, to almost $108 billion. Reflecting the weak nature of the banking recovery so far, this new record took seven years to achieve and required a $1.5 trillion, or 20 percent, increase in total assets, yet was only $5 billion above the pre-crisis record. Larger banks had the largest percentage increase in net income last year. Net income at banks with assets more than $1 billion increased 12 percent, while net income for banks with assets less than $1 billion increased by just 3 percent (see table 2).

Lower provision expense over the past year drove the improvement in profitability in banks of all sizes. Lower noninterest expense also supported profit growth for the largest banks. Net interest income remains under pressure from below-average loan growth and the low interest rate environment, though the multi-year compression in margin appears to have stabilized over the course of 2013.

Provision expenses declined over the past year across the industry, with the largest banks (those with assets greater than $10 billion) reporting a 45 percent reduction in provisions for loan losses. Those with assets between $1 billion and $10 billion had a 65 percent reduction in provision expenses, while those with less than $1 billion in assets saw a 50 percent reduction. Provision expenses for the system overall remain at historical lows relative to charge-offs and near their all-time lows as a share of total loans. Therefore, lower provision expenses are likely to provide a diminishing benefit to earnings performance going forward—assuming loan growth stays modest and ALLL ratios stabilize as expected.

Table 2: Income and Expenses

	Assets greater than $10 billion		Assets between $1 billion and $10 billion		Assets less than $1 billion	
	December 31, 2012	December 31, 2013	December 31, 2012	December 31, 2013	December 31, 2012	December 31, 2013
Number of institutions	60	58	184	165	1,615	1,427
Total assets in billions	8,870.0	9,347.6	493.5	452.4	372.8	340.6
Year-to-date revenues in $ billions						
Net interest income	262.0	259.0	14.0	13.8	10.8	10.6
Noninterest income	166.0	169.0	7.7	7.2	5.8	5.9
Realized securities gains and losses	6.0	3.0	0.2	0.1	0.2	0.1
Year-to-date expenses in $ billions						
Provisioning	40.0	22.0	1.7	0.6	1.0	0.5
Noninterest expense	266.0	259.0	14.7	14.9	11.6	11.9
Income taxes	39.0	49.0	1.4	0.9	1.0	1.0
Net income	89.0	100.0	4.2	4.7	3.1	3.2

Source: Integrated Banking Information System (OCC)

Note: Data are merger-adjusted and held constant for institutions in continuous operation from the first quarter of 2013 to the fourth quarter of 2013. Excludes credit card and trust institutions.

Return on Equity Improving, Led by Larger Banks

ROE generally improved in 2013 for banks with assets more than $10 billion and banks with assets less than $1 billion, but slipped slightly for banks with assets between $1 billion and $10 billion (see figure 5). Weighted-average ROE for all asset classes performed better than the median ROEs in 2013. This indicates that the largest banks within each of these groups are recovering at a more rapid pace than the typical banks in each of these groups. In particular, the smallest banks under $1 billion are seeing a significant degree of differentiation in profitability that was not seen before 2008, as those hit hardest by the recession continue to struggle, while approximately one-third are experiencing relatively rapid loan growth and much improved profits.

Figure 5: Return on Equity Trends by Bank Size

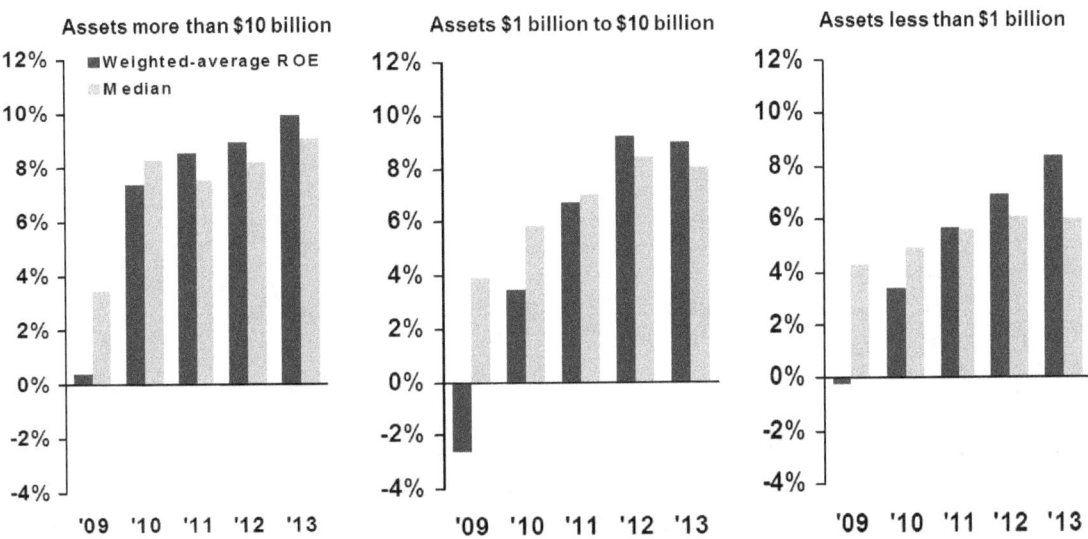

Source: Integrated Banking Information System (OCC)

Note: All data as of year-end. Sum-of-quarterly net income as a share of 5-quarter trailing average equity.

Noninterest Income Rising Slowly for Large and Small Banks

Although a much larger contributor for banks with assets more than $1 billion, the share of revenue from noninterest income rose only slightly for both large and small banks. Noninterest income, as a share of net operating revenue, increased to just over 40 percent for banks with assets greater than $1 billion and more than 24 percent for smaller institutions (see figure 6). Trading losses at large banks drove the big drop in 2008, but since 2011, trading revenue has helped push noninterest income higher as a share of total revenue. Asset management revenue also continues to provide a steady stream of noninterest income for some banks. Just as important, the ongoing decline in net interest income has contributed to the increased importance of noninterest income to bank revenue.

Figure 6: Trends in Noninterest Income

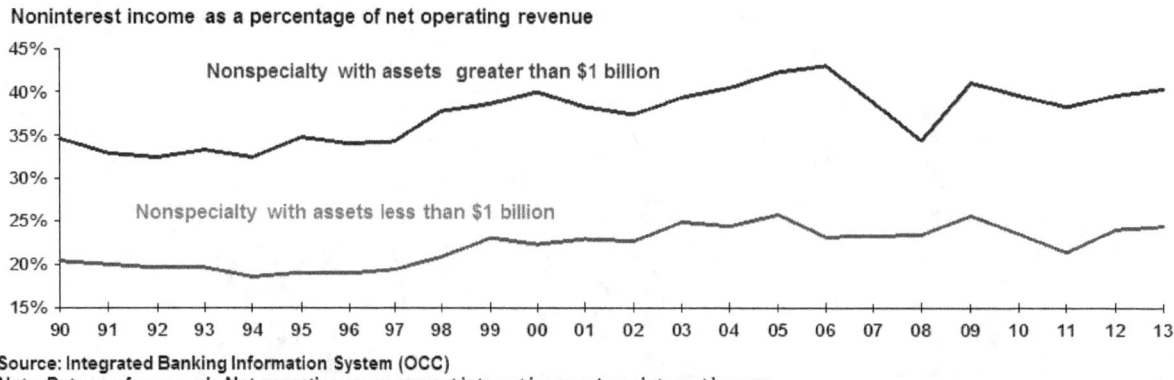

Noninterest income as a percentage of net operating revenue

Source: Integrated Banking Information System (OCC)
Note: Data as of year-end. Net operating revenue = net interest income + noninterest income

Trading Revenue Increased in 2013, but Masks a Weakening Trend

Banks reported $22.2 billion in trading revenue in 2013, $4.2 billion or 24 percent higher than the $18.0 billion reported in 2012 (see figure 7). Much of the improvement, however, was because of two large, nonrecurring events that depressed trading performance in 2012. First, a large bank incurred approximately $6 billion in well-publicized credit derivatives losses. Second, banks incurred much larger losses due to declines in their own credit spreads in 2012 than in 2013. Under accounting rules, lower bank credit spreads translate into higher derivatives liability fair values. Banks report these liability fair value adjustments as trading losses. Adjusting for these nonrecurring and noncore losses, trading revenue in 2013 would have been the lowest in three years. Indeed, there appears to be an emerging trend toward lower trading revenue, particularly in interest rate and foreign exchange products, the principal drivers of bank trading revenue.

Figure 7: Trading Revenue

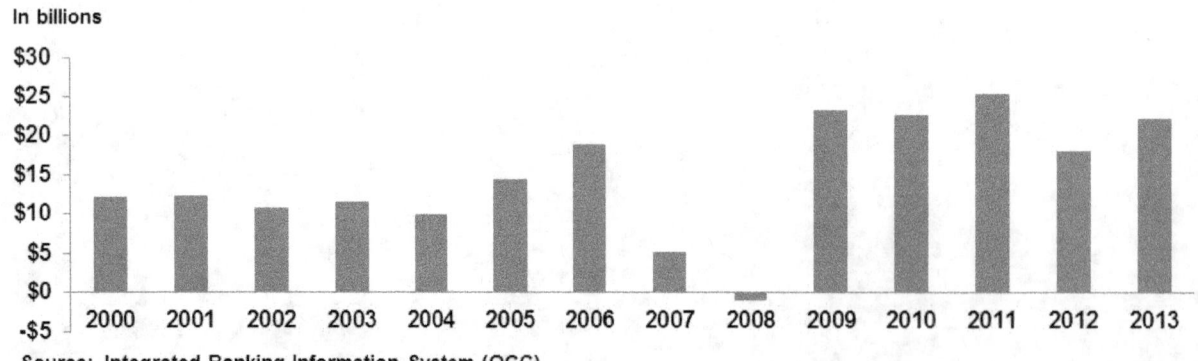

In billions

Source: Integrated Banking Information System (OCC).

The recent decline in trading revenue from interest rate and foreign exchange contracts illustrates more clearly the underlying weakness of trading revenue in 2013 (see figure 8).

Figure 8: Trading Revenue for Interest Rate and Foreign Exchange Contracts

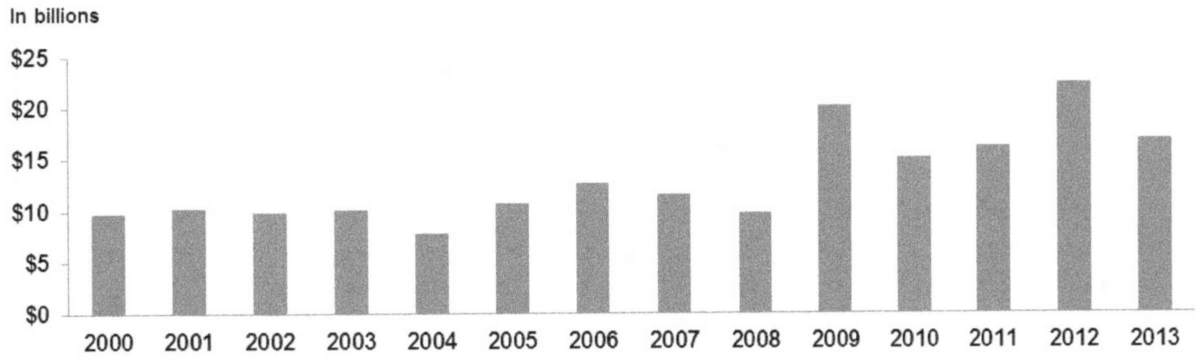

In billions

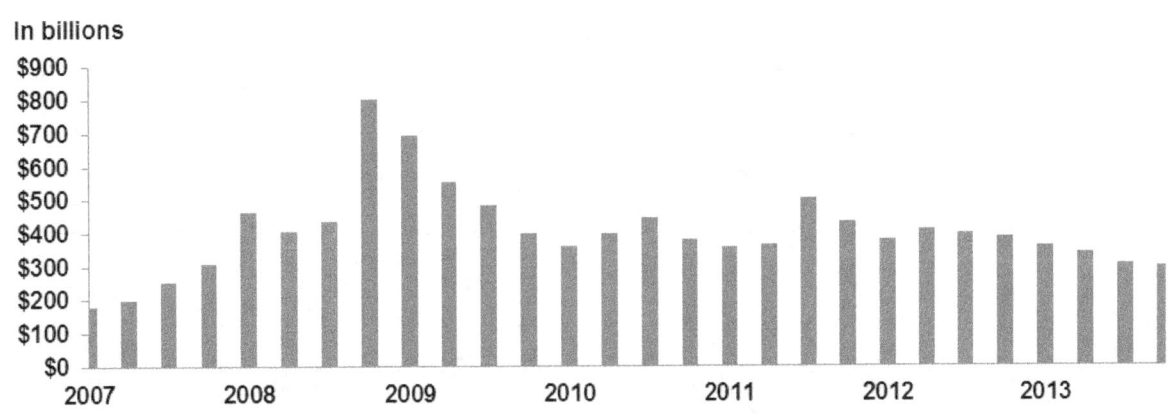

Source: Integrated Banking Information System (OCC).

Counterparty Credit Exposure From Derivatives Continues to Decline

Counterparty credit exposure from derivatives is a significant potential risk in trading activities. After peaking at $800 billion at the height of the financial crisis, net current credit exposure (NCCE), the primary metric the OCC uses to evaluate credit risk in bank derivatives activities, has declined steadily (see figure 9). NCCE is now at its lowest level since the end of 2007. NCCE is falling because the difference between current market swap rates and the contract rates in dealers' interest rate books has narrowed. Because interest rate contracts are 82 percent of total notional derivatives, credit exposure from derivatives is concentrated in interest rate exposures. The extended period of low interest rates, and the substantial growth in notional derivatives that has occurred during this low-rate period, have brought contract rates in dealer books more in line with current market levels. Banks hold high-quality collateral against 82 percent of NCCE.

Figure 9: Net Current Credit Exposure

In billions

Source: Integrated Banking Information System (OCC)

Central clearing mandates in the Dodd–Frank Act have led to a significant increase in centrally cleared derivatives transactions. A CCP reduces risks to participants in the derivatives and securities markets through multilateral netting of trades, imposing risk controls, and maintaining financial resources commensurate with the risks it carries. Central clearing allows market participants to face the credit risk of the CCP rather than each other, as the CCP acts as the buyer to every seller, and the seller to every buyer.

One consequence of increased central clearing is that credit risk that historically was more widely distributed on a bilateral basis has become concentrated in a small number of CCPs. The credit concentration inherent in CCPs, and the interconnectedness that results from having large entities as members of multiple CCPs, underscores the critical importance for CCPs to have robust capital requirements. Recently, a CCP in South Korea required members to contribute capital to cover a $45 million loss incurred due to a trade error that caused the failure of one of its members. This assessment of nondefaulting members highlights the mutualization of risk inherent in CCPs and illustrates the importance for members to understand the waterfall of losses. It also is a reminder that banks planning to join a CCP should undertake extensive due diligence to determine if the CCP has appropriate risk controls in place.

Low Market Volatility May Understate Risk

Unprecedented monetary policy easing has resulted in sharply lower interest rates, higher stock prices, and lower market volatility. Market volatility is a key factor in computing many risk measures. For example, banks use VaR models to measure the risk of trading activities. Aggregate VaR has dropped significantly since the end of the financial crisis at the five largest U.S. banking companies with trading operations (see figure 10). While some of the VaR decline is a result of lower client activity and reduced bank trading risk appetite, the low-volatility environment is the primary cause of lower VaR. In a more normal volatility environment, one without sustained monetary policy accommodation by the Federal Reserve, bank VaR would be meaningfully higher. Thus, current VaR calculations may understate trading risk in the banking system.

Figure 10: Aggregate Value-at-Risk at Five Large Banking Companies

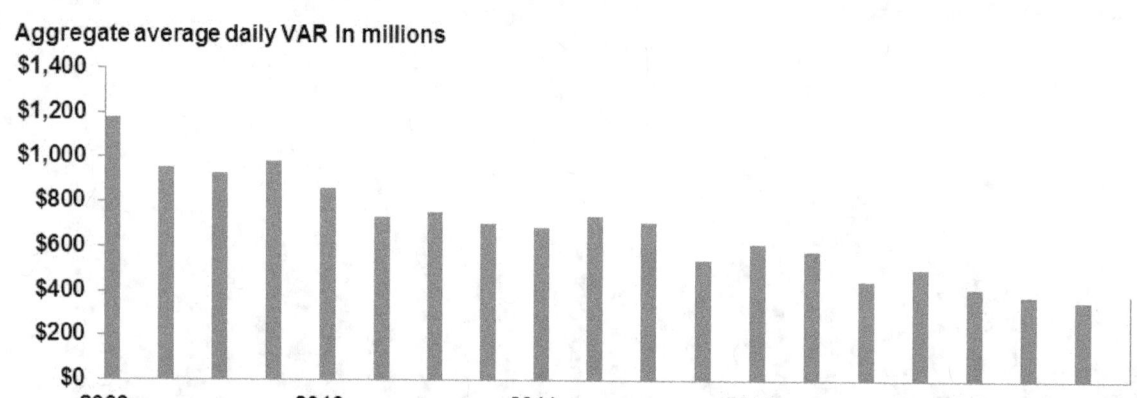

Aggregate average daily VAR In millions

Source: 10Q and 10 K Filings for Bank of America, JP Morgan Chase, Citigroup, Morgan Stanley, Goldman Sachs

Net Interest Margin Compression Continues

NIM remains under pressure as assets reprice at lower interest rates, but began to stabilize during 2013 (see figure 11). The low interest rate climate continues to limit the ability of many banks to increase net interest income through volume. Consumer and commercial loans with pricing tied to short-term indexes are unlikely to show improvement until the federal funds rate begins to increase. Accordingly, with the yield curve steepening, the incentive for banks to increase loan volume by loosening underwriting standards or investing excess cash into longer-maturity securities has increased, potentially increasing banks' exposure to credit risk and IRR.

Figure 11: Trends in Net Interest Margins

Net interest margin as a percentage of earning assets

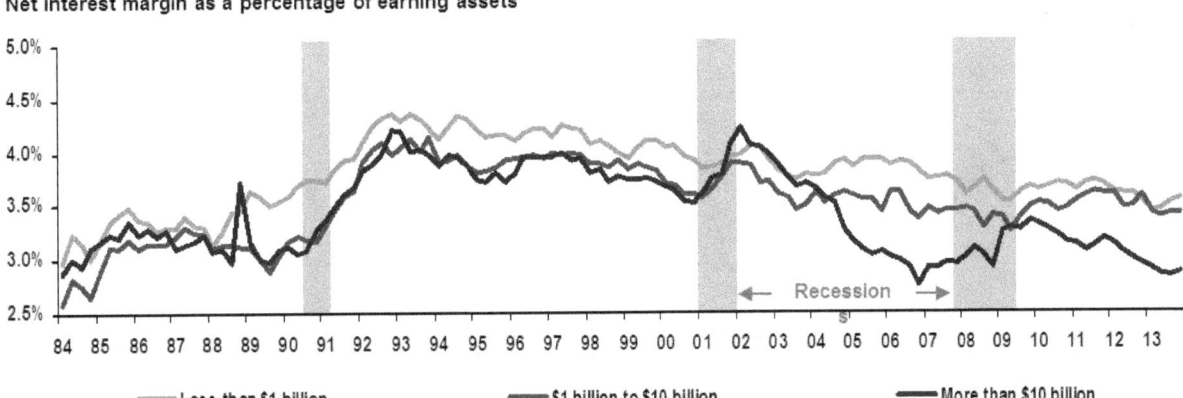

Source: Integrated Banking Information System (OCC)

Note: Quarterly data through the fourth quarter of 2013. Nonspecialty category excludes credit card and trust banks.

B. Loan Growth Challenges

Total Loan Growth: C&I-Driven at Large Banks; Regionally Uneven for Small Banks

While slowly improving, loan growth remained below average during 2013. Loan growth remains centered in commercial loans, with the larger banks reporting more consistent loan growth. The median year-over-year loan growth rate for total loans was just over 4 percent for banks with assets more than $10 billion and 6 percent for banks with assets between $1 billion and $10 billion. Banks with total assets of less than $1 billion had a weaker 2 percent year-over-year loan growth. In 2013, median loan growth rates for banks of all sizes were well below their corresponding long-term growth averages (see figure 12).

Figure 12: Median Loan Growth Trends

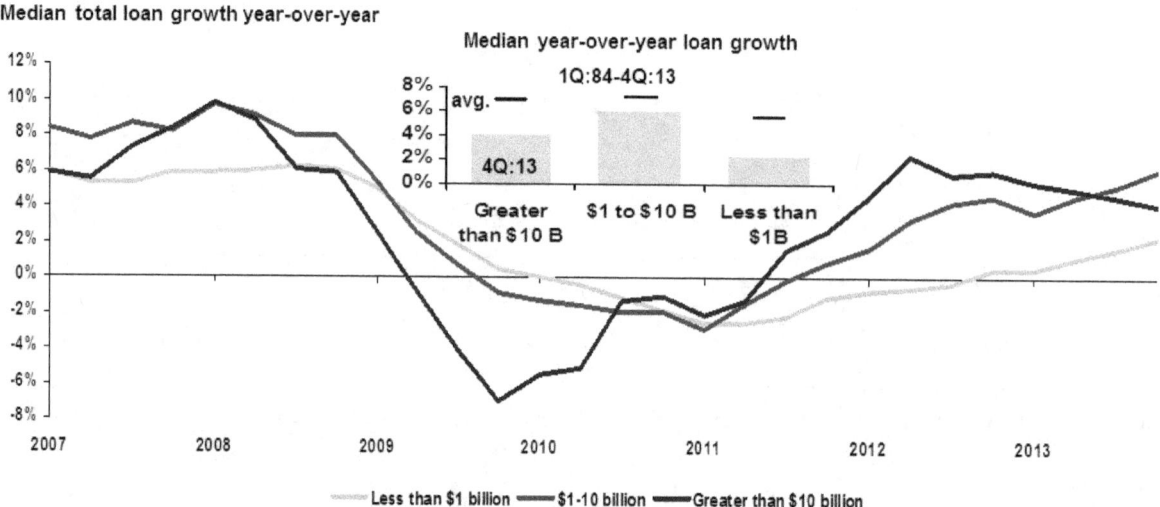

Source: Integrated Banking Information System (OCC)

Aggregate growth in C&I lending remains strong, though centered in larger banks. C&I lending growth in 2013 of almost 6 percent remains above the long-term average, but below the current cycle's approximate 16 percent peak in 2011. C&I loans outstanding at the end of 2013 were the highest since 2008 after a sharp contraction during the recession in 2009 (see figure 13).

Figure 13: C&I Loan Growth Trends

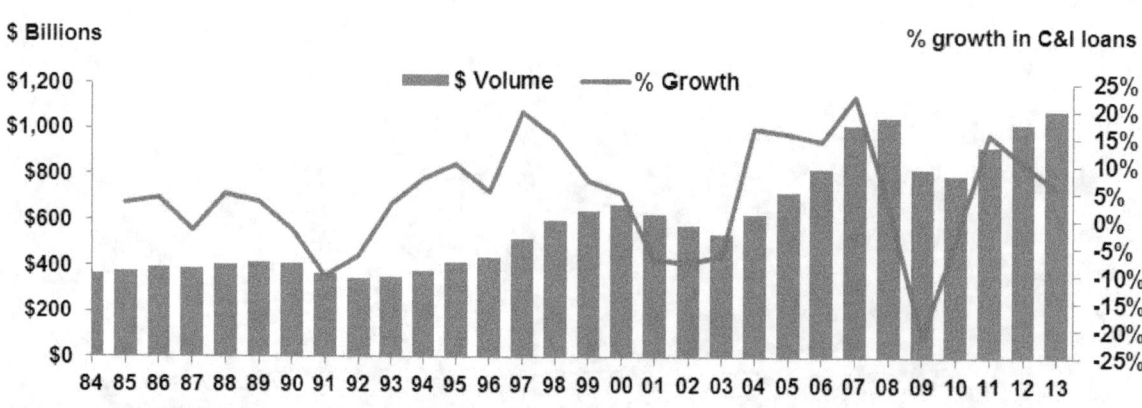

Source: Integrated Banking Information System (OCC)
Note: All data as of year-end.

C&I loans continue to be a large contributor to total loan growth for banks of all sizes (see figure 14). Loan demand from larger firms, fueled by improving business opportunities, continues to grow. Larger banks provide most of the credit support for these firms, and accordingly, have benefited most consistently from this trend. Smaller banks typically lend to small businesses, whose performance still lags behind larger corporations, and C&I loan growth at small banks has been more uneven. Some small banks are reporting robust C&I loan growth, while others continue to show declines. As of December 2013, and after adjusting for mergers, banks with less than $1 billion in assets as a group reported 2.4 percent growth in total loans outstanding over the past year, in part because of the bifurcation in small banks' loan activity.

Figure 14: Loan Growth Trends, Fourth Quarter 2012 to Fourth Quarter 2013

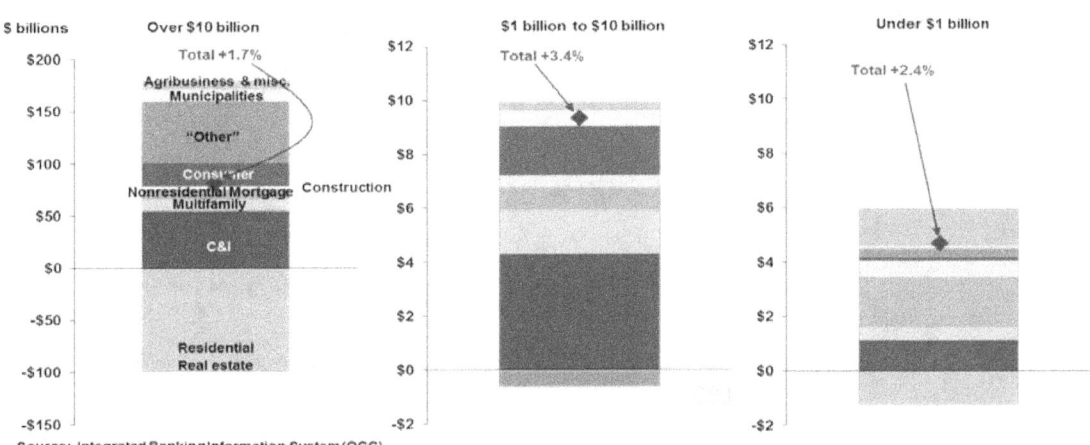

Source: Integrated Banking Information System (OCC)
Data are merger-adjusted and held constant for institutions in continuous operation from the fourth quarter of 2012 to fourth quarter of 2013
Note: Scales differ

The weak and uneven recovery in C&I growth at smaller banks is part of a broader pattern in their lending trends. Loan growth among small banks has not been as widespread as in normal economic times (see figure 15). On a regional basis, only 40 percent to 50 percent of banks with less than $1 billion in assets reported loan growth over the past year, compared with a more normal figure of 80 percent. Furthermore, growth varies widely by region, whereas it was more uniform in the past. The regions where small-bank loan growth remains weak include the mid-Atlantic states, Florida, and Georgia. Meanwhile, the Northeast, the Southern states except Florida and Georgia, and the Plains states are seeing some of the highest loan growth at small institutions. Local economic conditions drive these patterns, as strong agriculture and energy production have boosted local economies in certain states, while lingering real estate problems continue to weigh disproportionately on other regions.

Figure 15: Loan Growth for Small Banks by Region

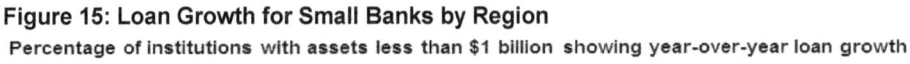

Percentage of institutions with assets less than $1 billion showing year-over-year loan growth

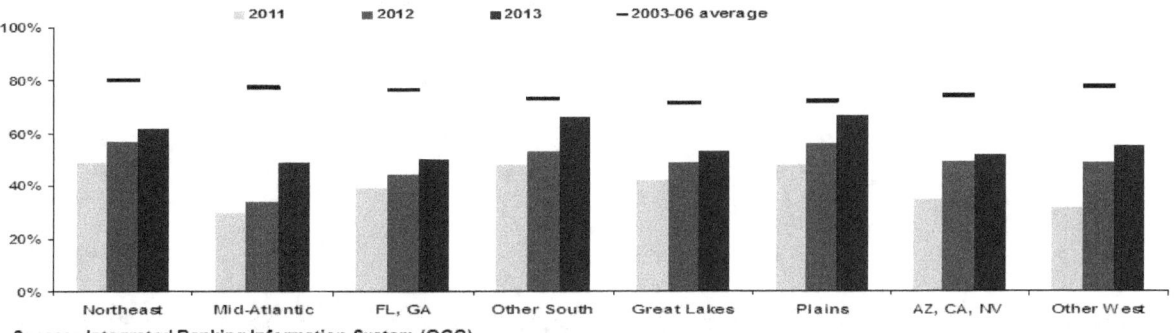

Source: Integrated Banking Information System (OCC)

Northeast = CT, MA, ME, NH, NJ, NY, PA, RI, VT   Mid-Atlantic = DC, DE, MD, NC, SC, VA, WV
Great Lakes = IL, IN, MI, OH, WI   Plains = IA, KS, MN, MO, ND, NE, SD
Other South = AL, AR, KY, LA, MS, TN, TX, OK   Other West = AK, CO, HI, ID, MT, NM, OR, UT, WA, WY

Commercial Loan Growth Led by Finance and Insurance, Real Estate, and Energy

Banks reporting to the OCC's Credit Analytics data system (accounting for over 80 percent of total commercial loan commitments in the federal banking system)[6] experienced growth in commercial commitments exceeding 7.1 percent, or $263 billion, in 2013. While credit growth was evident across most industry groups, lending to finance and insurance (nonbank financials), real estate and construction, and energy led the way (see figure 16). Among the nonbank finance and insurance industries, the fastest growth is shown by funds and other financial vehicles. The strongest growth within real estate lending was commercial mortgages to owners and lessors of residential property, mainly apartments. Lending to the oil, gas, and coal industry has grown steadily, even during the recession years, and is a new area of focus for many banks. Other industry groups with strong double-digit growth include automobile-related (principally auto parts and auto dealers), media and telecommunications, food and drug stores, and professional services. The OCC continues to emphasize the need for banks to ensure that they have the necessary expertise to understand the risks in these industries.

Figure 16: Commercial Loan Growth by Industry for Reporting Banks

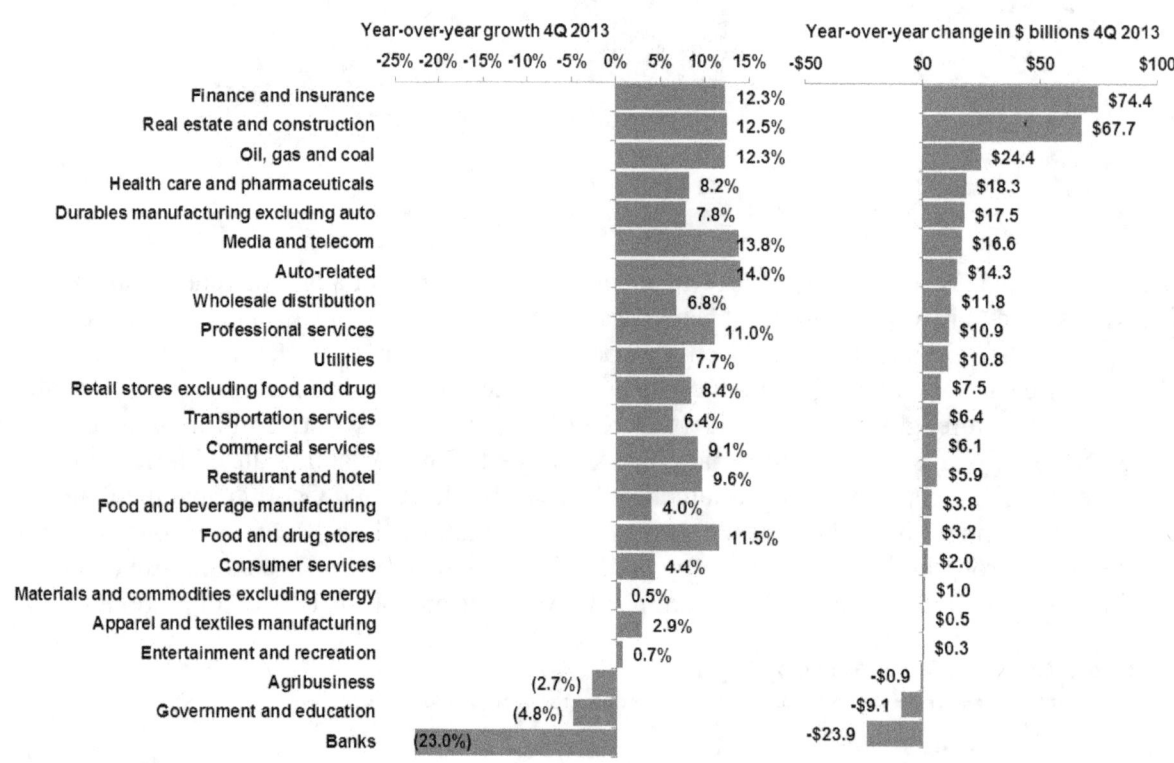

Source: OCC Credit Analytics

---

[6] Credit Analytics is an OCC-sponsored, voluntary data-sharing program for analyzing commercial credit trends. The participants represent a substantial share of total commercial lending by the federal banking system.

Retail Lending Turns Positive, Driven Mostly by Autos and Student Loans

For the first time since mid-2008, consumer credit showed two consecutive quarters of growth. Overall, retail credit outstandings totaled $12.96 trillion at the end of 2013, $110 billion more than the 2012 level but almost $1 trillion below the peak in June 2008. The increase was largely from strong growth in auto lending and student debt, along with the first increase in residential mortgage balances in five years. Retail loan balances in OCC-supervised banks, however, have declined on a year-over-year basis for 21 consecutive quarters, as banks are not substantial lenders in the student loan markets (see figure 17).

Figure 17: Quarterly Trends in Retail Credit Growth

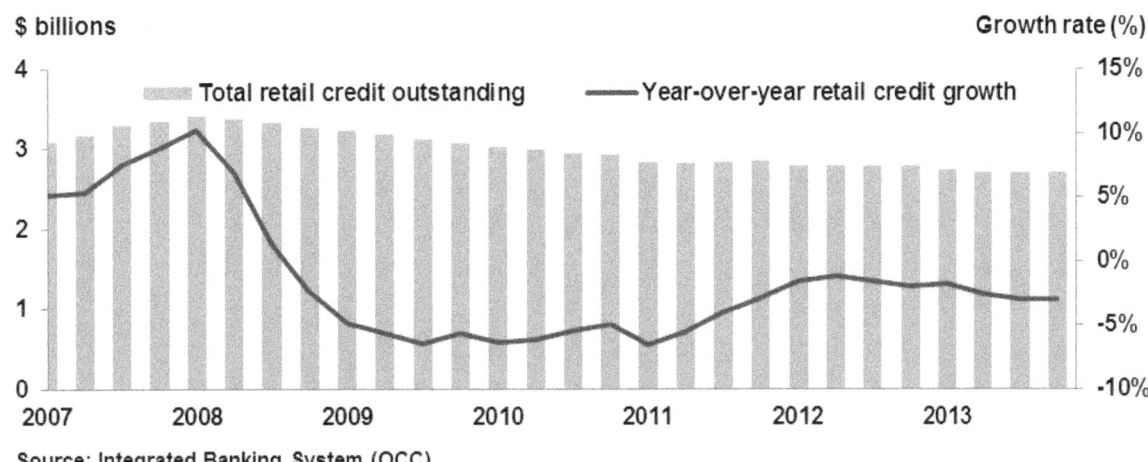

Source: Integrated Banking System (OCC)

Auto lending remained a highly competitive product segment, as strong growth continued through the end of 2013. Banks reported year-over-year growth of 11.3 percent in the third quarter of 2013 and 12.9 percent in the fourth quarter of 2013 (see figure 18). Banks continue to hold a sizable market share of outstanding loans of $250 billion, or 31 percent of the total auto lending market. In part III of this report, we note signs of increasing risk for auto lending that are common in competitive markets where growth is accelerating. We will continue to monitor this market closely.

Figure 18: Quarterly Trends in Auto Loans

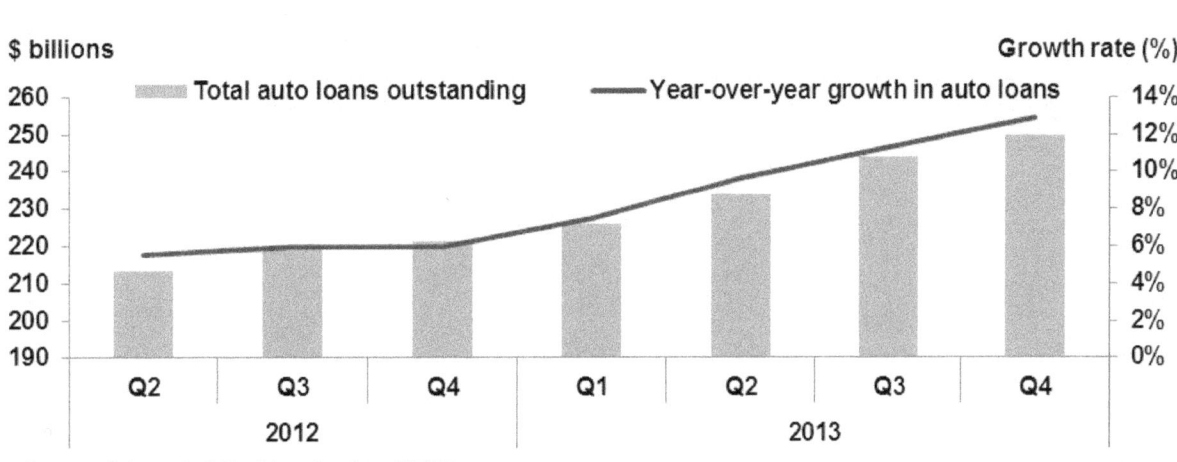

Source: Integrated Banking System (OCC)

Residential Mortgage Runoff Has Slowed as Foreclosure Activity Declines

A decline in new foreclosure activity helped offset slowing mortgage origination activity in 2013. Both foreclosure inventory and foreclosure starts are improving as backlogs ease and fewer new proceedings begin. New foreclosure starts are down in the prime and subprime segments, indicating a slow but broadening housing market stabilization. It is also attributed to improved economic conditions and aggressive foreclosure prevention actions (see figure 19). Mortgage originations started out strong in 2013, but rising interest rates beginning in May caused origination activity to wane. With only gradual improvement in economic fundamentals such as job and income growth and household formation, incremental demand for mortgages remains low.

Figure 19: Trend in U.S. Foreclosure Starts

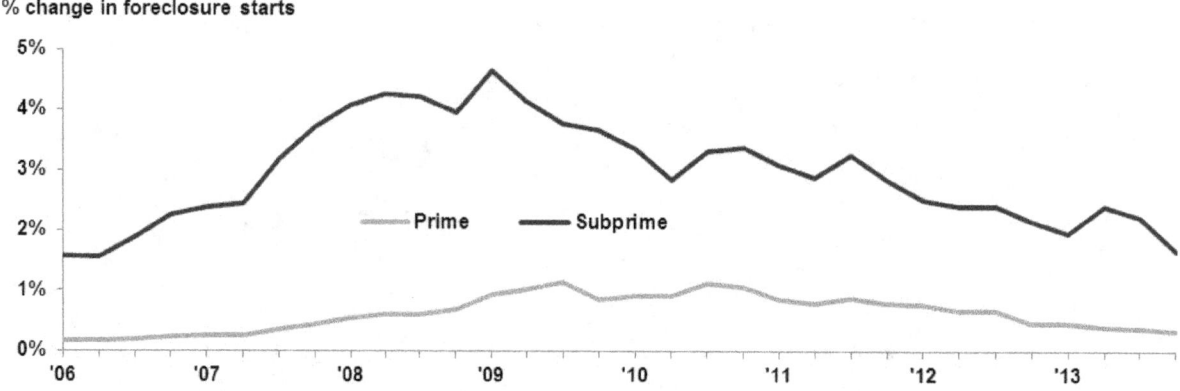

Source: Mortgage Bankers Association, Haver
Note: Data from first quarter of 2006 through the fourth quarter of 2013.

C. Credit Quality: Significant Improvement in Key Risk Metrics in 2013

Credit Metrics Continue to Improve, but Noncurrent Loans Remain High

As they have for the past several years, key credit risk metrics improved in 2013 (see figure 20). Total noncurrent loans—those 90 days or more past due or on nonaccrual—declined for large and small banks, but remain stubbornly high. Net charge-offs have declined to near pre-crisis levels. The ALLL as a percentage of total loans also declined as credit quality improved. The OCC expects the pace of the decline in the ALLL ratio to abate as it returns to a more normal share of total loans. Because noncurrent loans remain historically elevated and the economic outlook remains guarded, the ALLL-to-total-loan ratio may stabilize above its pre-crisis level.

Figure 20: Credit Cycle Analysis

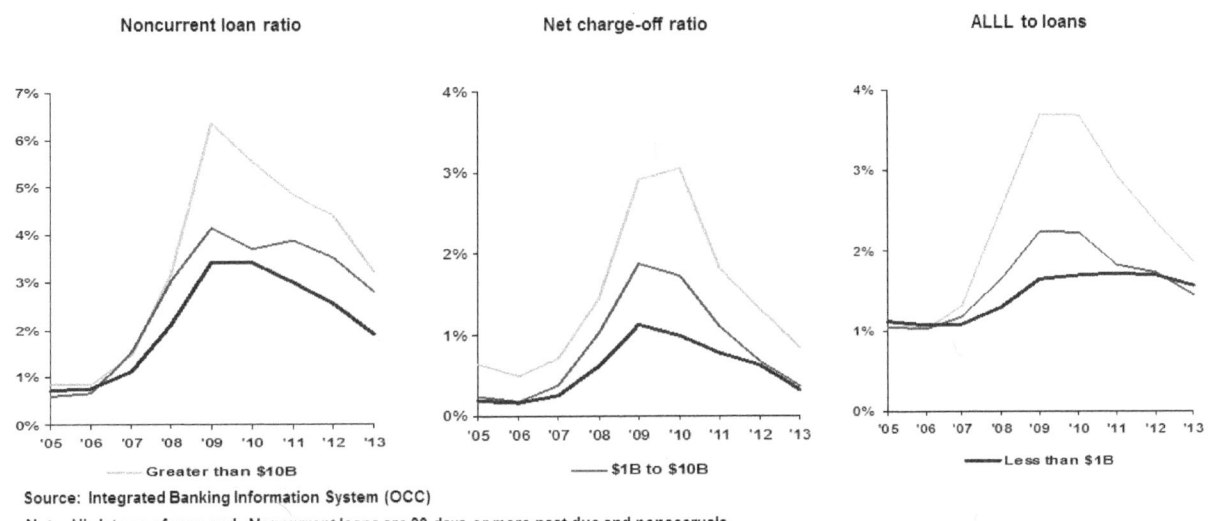

Source: Integrated Banking Information System (OCC)

Note: All data as of year-end. Noncurrent loans are 90-days or more past due and nonaccruals.

Charge-Off Rates for Most Loan Types Drop Below Long-Term Averages

Charge-off rates continued their decline through the end of 2013 for all major loan types (see figure 21). The current loss rate levels for all major loan types except HELOCs and one- to four-family residential have dropped below the post-1990 long-term average.

Figure 21: Charge-Off Rates by Asset Class

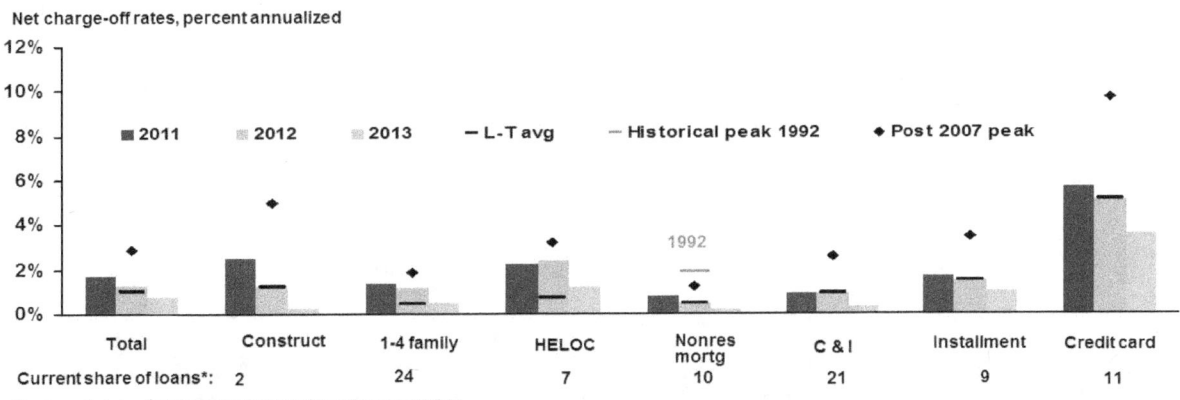

Source: Integrated Banking Information System (OCC)

* Not all detail loan categories are shown. Net charge-offs as a percent of loans in respective category.

Commercial Loan Quality Improved

The level of classified loans, their weighted-average probability of default, and key qualitative credit metrics all declined in 2013, reflecting the much-improved condition of commercial loan portfolios (see figure 22). The OCC's Credit Analytics data also show consistent, moderate growth in commercial loan commitments during 2013.

Figure 22: Commercial Loan Trends for Select Banks

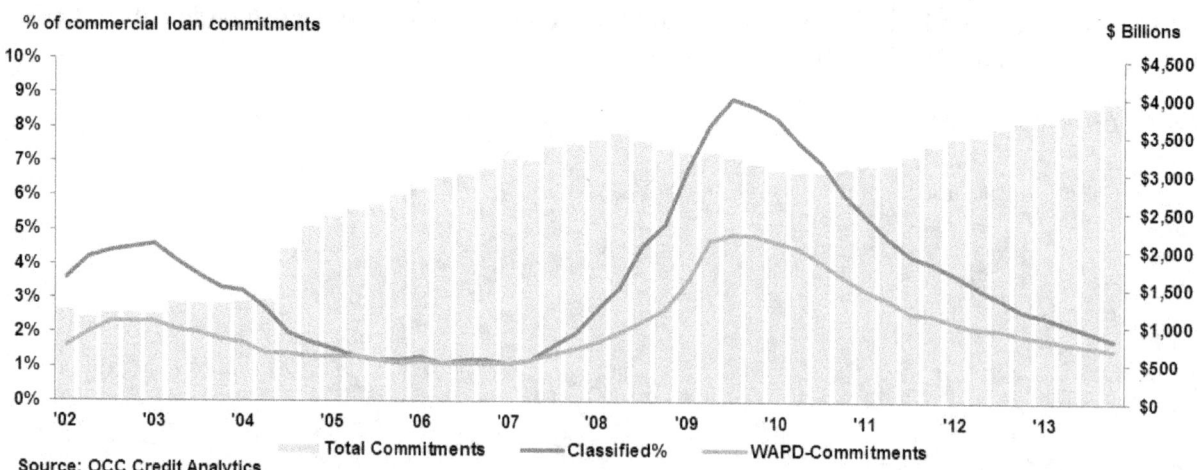

Source: OCC Credit Analytics
Note: WAPD = Weighted-average probability of default to commitments

Part III: Key Risk Issues

A. Competition Drives Easing in Underwriting Standards

Significant Growth in Leveraged Loans Accompanied by Weaker Underwriting

U.S. syndicated leveraged loan issuance reached a record high in 2013 as the search for yield in the low interest rate environment drove an increase in risk appetite across institutional investors such as collateralized loan obligations (CLO) and retail loan funds (see figure 23). Issuers continued to take advantage of low interest rates, and competition among lenders for new business remained intense. Merger and acquisition loans had a strong year (32 percent of new issuance) and achieved the highest issuance volume since 2007, driven by higher corporate profit margins and business valuations. The average total-debt-to-EBITDA (earnings before interest, taxes, depreciation, and amortization) multiple for leveraged loans issued in 2013 rose to 4.7X, a level last exceeded in 2007 (see figure 23). The combination of higher leverage, lower yields, tighter credit spreads, and weaker covenant protections provides ample evidence of increasing credit risk in the leveraged loan market.

Figure 23: Average Total Debt-to-EBITDA Multiples and U.S. Leveraged Loan Volume

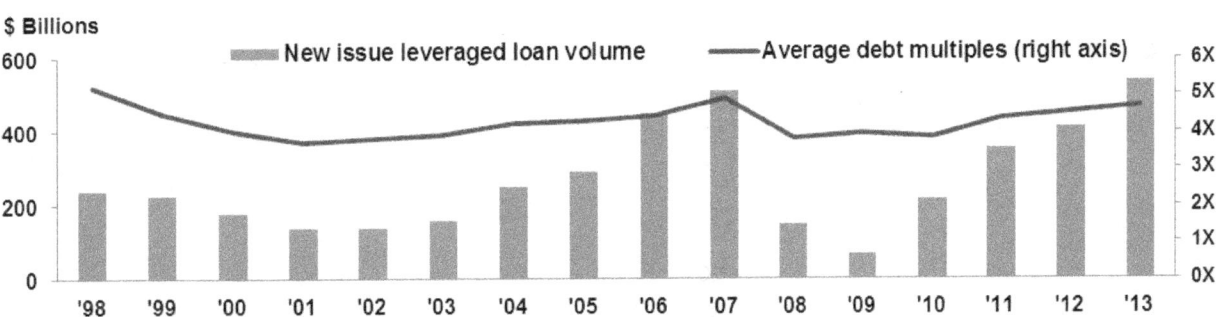

Source: Standard & Poor's LCD. All data as of year-end.
Note: Excludes Existing Tranches of Add-ons and Amendments & Restatements with No New Money
S&P and its third-party providers are not liable for errors or omissions in the data/information and the context from which it is drawn.

Volume of New-Issue Covenant-Lite Leveraged Loans Surges

Investor demand for high-yield products continued to surge, with more relaxed structures incorporating fewer covenants and lender protections. New-issue covenant-lite loans totaled $258 billion in 2013, nearly equal to the total cumulative amount issued from 1997 to 2012 (see figure 24). Accordingly, the quality of underwriting in the syndicated leveraged loan market remains a supervisory concern.

Figure 24: New Issuance of Covenant-Lite Leveraged Loans

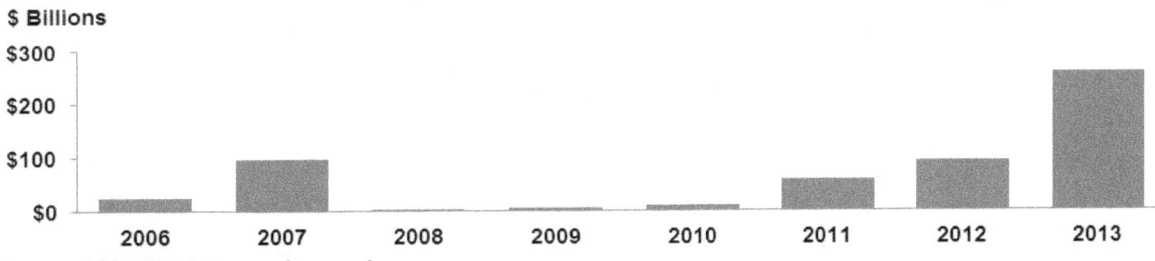

Source: S&P LCD. All data as of year-end.
Note: Excludes Existing Tranches of Add-ons and Amendments & Restatements with No New Money
S&P and its third-party providers are not liable for errors or omissions in the data/information and the context from which it is drawn.

Loan Underwriting Standards Easing

The OCC's Survey of Credit Underwriting Practices (issued January 30, 2014, based on data as of June 30, 2013) show that underwriting standards are easing in both commercial and retail products, as banks adapt to changing economic conditions and competition. The largest OCC-supervised banks reported the highest share of eased underwriting standards among various size groups. Examiners cited large banks' increasing risk appetite, intense competition, and market liquidity as factors driving the easing of standards. Loan portfolios that experienced the most easing in standards included indirect consumer, credit cards, large corporate, ABL, international, and leveraged loans. Changes in collateral requirements, loosening covenants, and scorecard cutoffs were the primary methods that banks used to ease standards. Loan portfolios with the most tightening in underwriting included high loan-to-value (LTV) home equity and conventional home equity.

The Federal Reserve Board's January 2014 "Senior Loan Officer Opinion Survey on Bank Lending Practices" reported continued net easing of lending policies and underwriting standards on C&I and CRE loans in the fourth quarter of 2013. The survey reported net easing of lending standards for eight consecutive quarters for both C&I and CRE (see figure 25). Aggressive competition from banks and nonbank lenders and an improving economic climate were among the reasons cited for the net easing of standards. Most of the easing was reported in loan covenants, maturity, and pricing.

Figure 25: Percentage of Survey Respondents Tightening C&I and CRE Underwriting Standards

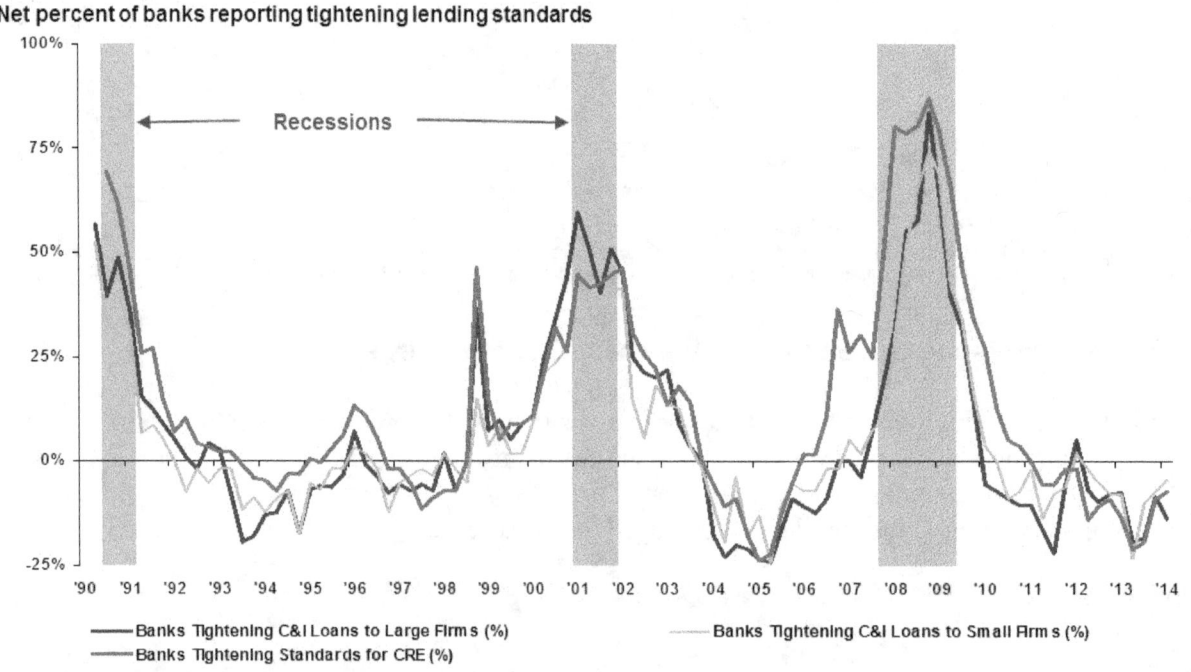

Net percent of banks reporting tightening lending standards

Source: Federal Reserve Board/Haver Analytics (January 2014)

Signs of Risk in Auto Lending Beginning to Emerge

Across the industry, auto lenders are pursuing growth by lengthening terms, increasing advance rates, and originating loans to borrowers with lower credit scores. Loan marketing has become increasingly monthly-payment driven, with loan terms and LTV advance rates easing to make financing more broadly available. The results have yet to show large-scale deterioration at the portfolio level, but signs of increasing risk are evident. Average LTV rates for both new and used vehicles are above 100 percent for all major lender categories, reflecting rising car prices and a greater bundling of add-on products such as extended warranties, credit life insurance, and aftermarket accessories into the financing (see figure 26).

Figure 26: Average LTV by Lender

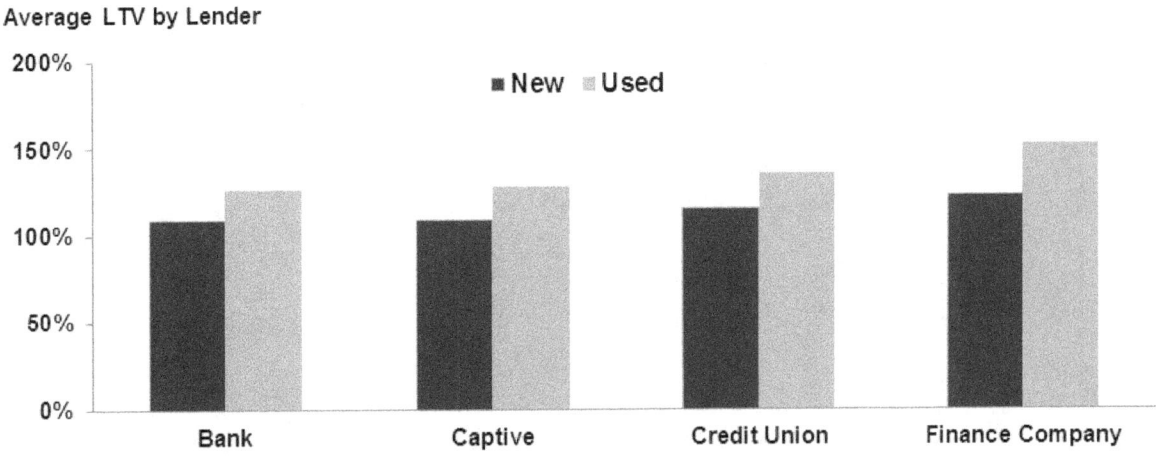

Average LTV by Lender

Source: Experian, *State of the Automotive Finance Market* 4Q2013

The average loss per vehicle has risen substantially in the past two years, an indication of how longer terms and higher LTVs can increase exposure. Average charge-off amounts are higher across all lender types over the last year (see figure 27). These early signs of easing terms and increasing risk are noteworthy, and the OCC will continue to monitor product terms and risk layering practices to ensure that banks manage growth and exposure prudently.

Figure 27: Average Charge-off Amount by Lender

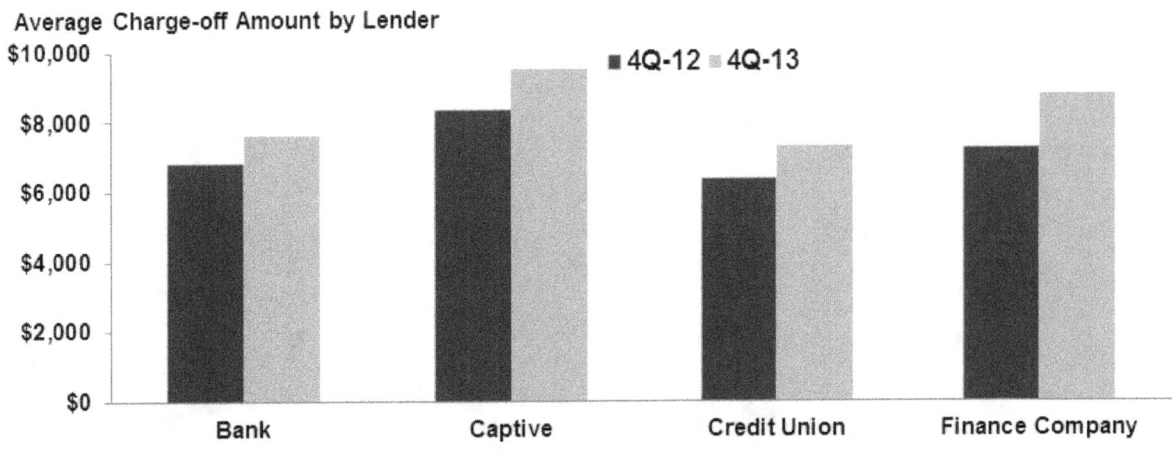

Average Charge-off Amount by Lender

Source: Experian, *State of the Automotive Finance Market* 4Q2013

B. HELOC Risk Easing

HELOC End-of-Draw Risk is Significant, but Volumes Have Declined

HELOC exposure is declining, but significant volumes are still scheduled to reach end-of-draw periods between 2014 and 2018. HELOC volumes approaching end-of-draw between 2011 and 2013 at the nine largest OCC-regulated banks declined (see figure 28). The declining volumes reflect normal attrition and active risk management efforts to address HELOC exposures. While improving, substantial challenges remain, and the OCC will continue to monitor exposure levels and lender efforts to mitigate the risks.

Figure 28: HELOC End-of-Draw Volume

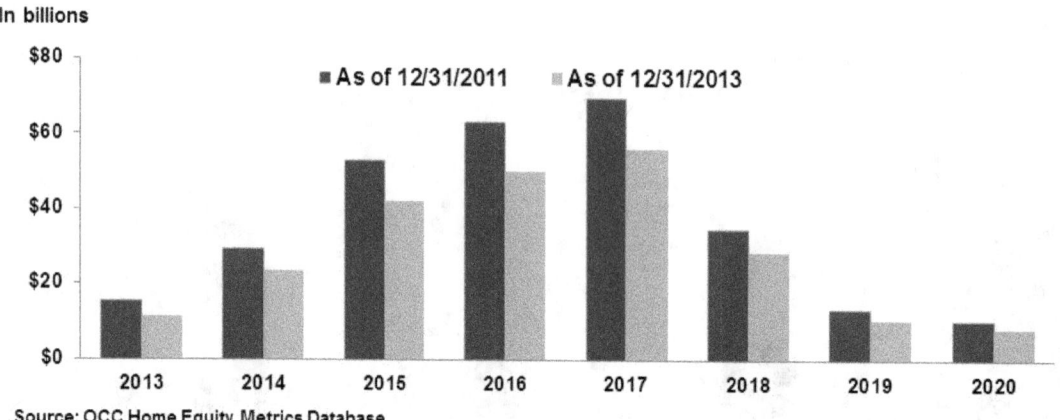

Source: OCC Home Equity Metrics Database

C. Interest Rate Risk Vulnerabilities

Retention Rate of Post-Crisis Core Deposit Growth Remains Uncertain

The retention rate (and pricing) of post-crisis deposits remains a key behavioral factor in IRR models. The surge in deposits associated with the flight to quality that began during the financial crisis has continued (see figure 29). This trend is supported by the near-zero rate environment and the fact that low rates make it inexpensive for depositors to remain liquid. Segments of a bank's core depositors may react differently in an increasing interest rate environment than they have in a low rate environment. Accordingly, the OCC will emphasize the need to analyze core deposits carefully, as some are potentially more sensitive to rising interest rates than historical relationships may suggest. Recent communications with the industry and ongoing IRR supervisory efforts have focused on deposit pricing and runoff assumptions in stressed rate environments. Deposit modeling assumptions are a key component of IRR measurements and a driver of earnings and economic capital exposures in modeled rate scenarios. Many banks are using deposit assumptions that are not well supported or are overly reliant on either customer behavior before the crisis or behavior since the surge in volume since the crisis. IRR data collection efforts have revealed a wide dispersion in non-maturity deposit assumptions. At a minimum, the OCC expects banks to model alternative deposit assumptions to test the potential effect on earnings and economic capital at risk from changes in interest rates.

Figure 29: Trends in Core Deposits for Banks

Core deposits**, excluding small CDs share of liabilities, percent

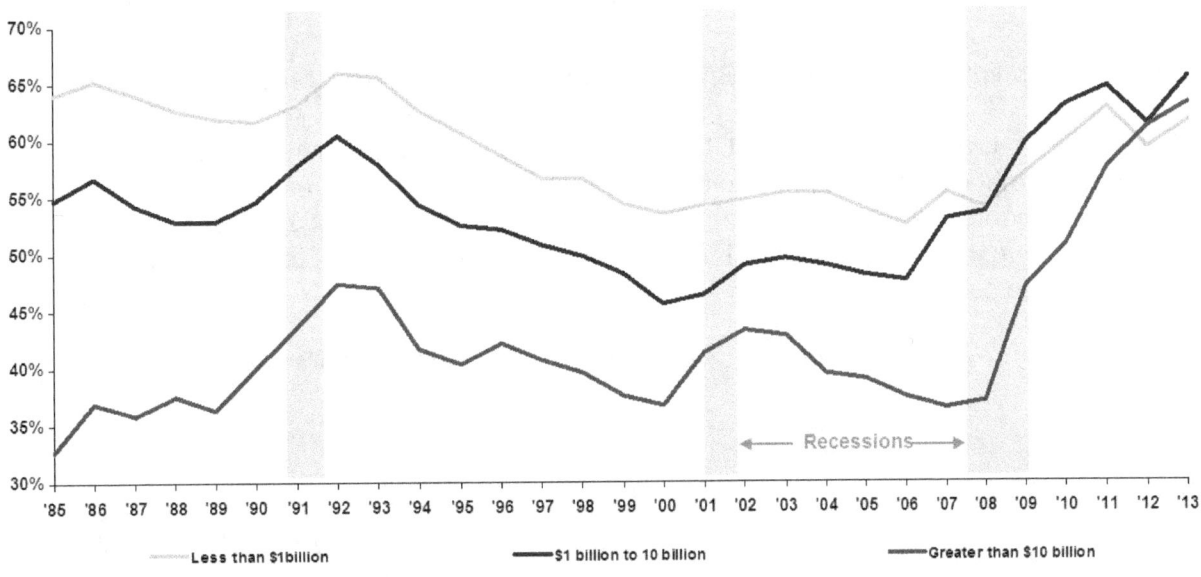

Source: Integrated Banking Information System (OCC)

Note: Data are as of year-end. **Core deposits defined as domestic deposits less time deposits of $100k or more. Ratio also excludes small CDs.

Small Banks' Investment Portfolios Concentrated in Mortgage-Backed Securities

Banks with assets less than $10 billion increased their aggregate investment portfolios since the 2008 crisis, primarily because of strong deposit inflows, uneven loan growth, and continued pressure on NIM (see figure 30). The increase in investment portfolios remains centered in MBS. Material concentrations in MBS could make some banks more vulnerable to IRR because of the potential for duration extension in a rising rate environment.

Figure 30: Investment Portfolio Mix for Banks With Total Assets Less Than $10 Billion

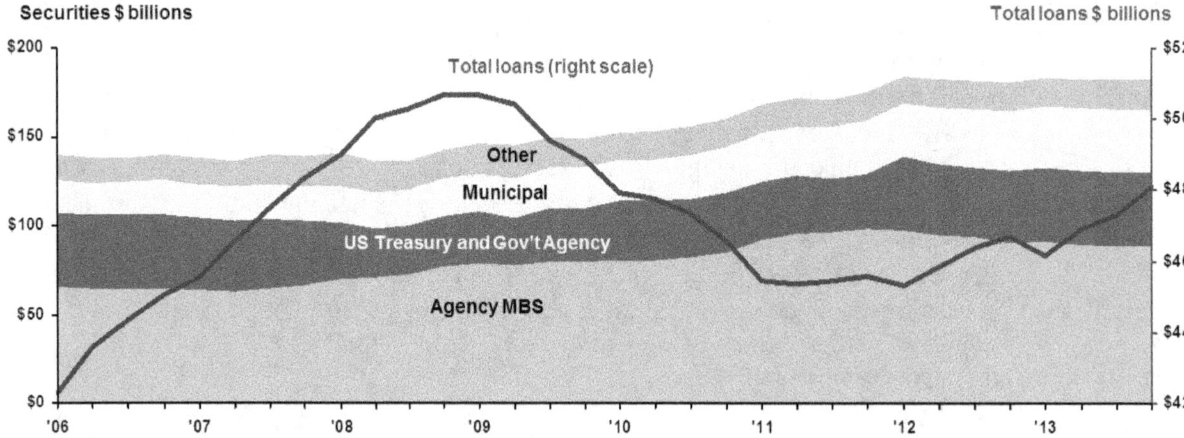

Source: Integrated Banking Information System (OCC)

Data are merger-adjusted and held constant for institutions in continuous operation from the first quarter of 2006 to the fourth quarter of 2013.

National Banks with Less Than $1 Billion in Assets Increasing Long-Term Assets

Extension risk is increasing for banks with less than $1 billion in assets as they search for yield by adding exposure to long-term assets. National banks with less than $1 billion in assets increased long-term asset concentrations from 17 percent in 2006 to 31 percent at the end of 2013 (see figure 31). In attempting to improve their NIM, national banks have increasingly relied on long-term assets with a focus on mortgage products.

Figure 31: Long-Term Asset Concentrations for National Banks with Less Than $1 Billion in Assets

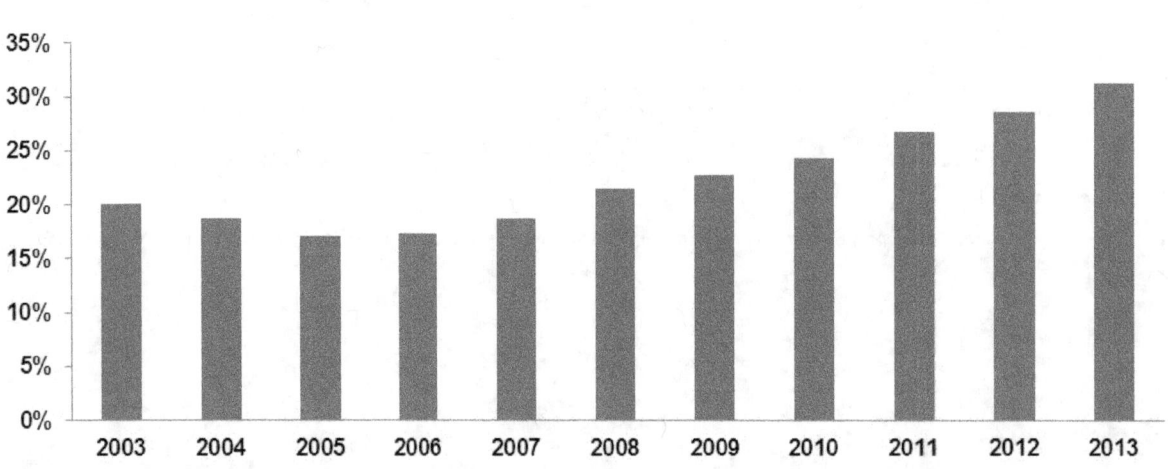

Source: Integrated Banking Information System (OCC)

D. Operational Risk Remains Elevated

Operational Risk Concentrated in the Largest Banks, but Increasing in Small Banks

Operational risk is elevated due to the amount and pace of internal and externally initiated change, greater interconnectedness and interdependencies that introduce information security and concentration vulnerabilities, and evolving and increased sophistication of cyber-threats. While high operational risk has been primarily concentrated in the largest banks, operational risk is increasing in midsize and community banks.

Several large and a small number of midsize banks continue to incur large legal settlements and regulatory penalties. Aggregate legal fees and settlements remain on an upward trend and are at a 10-year high (see figure 32). Securities and Exchange Commission reporting as of year-end 2013 indicates that the 12 largest bank holding companies (BHC) estimate maximum potential legal exposure of approximately $23 billion in excess of reserves. The exposure amounts were $14 billion and $20 billion for 2011 and 2012, respectively.

Figure 32: Trends in Legal Fees and Settlements

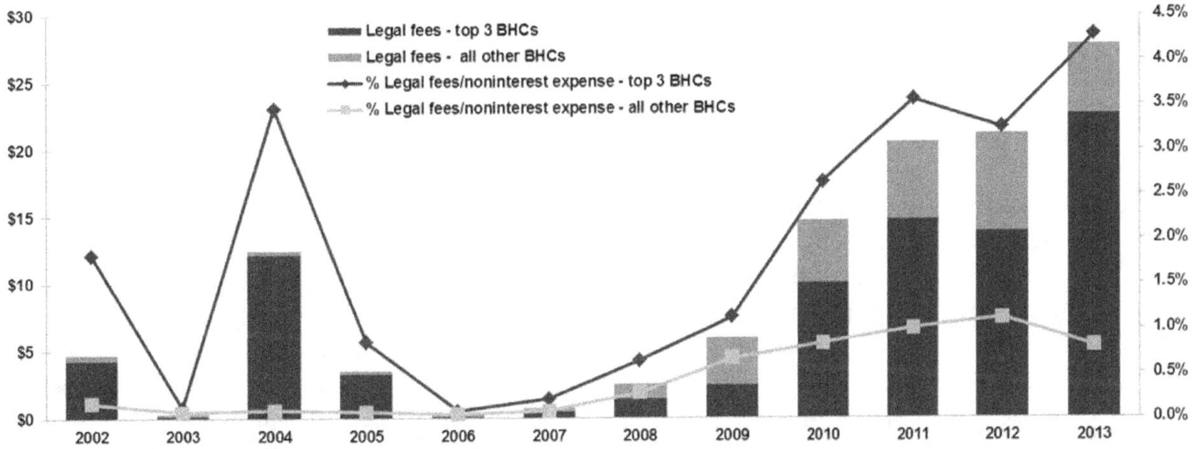

Source: Federal Reserve Y-9C Reports

Part IV: Elevated Risk Metrics

The OCC's NRC tracks a number of risk metrics to help monitor and communicate system-level financial risks to internal OCC audiences, including its examination staff, and to the industry. The group of indicators monitored by the NRC is starting to show some movement toward an increased risk appetite, following several years of risk aversion. This is especially evident in some of the underwriting indicators and other areas of concern discussed in this report. An increased risk appetite by itself is not generally a supervisory concern, provided banks maintain effective governance frameworks.

The NRC developed these indicators, some of which are below, by identifying their ability to provide signals of elevated risks during past economic cycles. These indicators are based on a contrarian view of risk—that is, they look for signals of unusually benign economic and market conditions. Historically, under such conditions, many bankers and investors begin to increase their risk appetites. For example, the following figures show that before the financial crisis of 2008, market volatility was very low, home prices were quickly increasing, and traditional credit indicators showed little risk. In that environment, many bankers increased their risk appetite because they assumed these indicators would remain positive. These indicators, when viewed collectively, help inform supervisory policy early in the credit cycle by providing a gauge of shifting risk appetite relative to historical levels—long before any potential negative consequences from these shifts become evident in lagging indicators, such as rising delinquency rates.

VIX and MOVE Indexes Signal Low Volatility

The VIX, a popular measure of the implied volatility of Standard & Poor's 500 index options, illustrates the general downward trend in volatility in recent years (see figure 33). Many market participants refer to the VIX as a "fear index" because it measures market expectations of near-term volatility, which tend to rise when market prices fall. VIX levels below 20 (and especially below 15) suggest complacency in the stock market, which often has led to sustained increases in risk appetite and subsequent market instability. Volatility moved higher in the second quarter of 2013, after the Federal Reserve suggested that it might begin to "taper" bond purchases (as it ultimately did begin to do later in the year). Volatility remains low by historic standards, however. The longer volatility remains low, the more likely investors are to chase yields to maximize returns, often selling options that expose them to losses if prices drop suddenly, or taking on increased credit risk. Accordingly, it is important that banks and investors take special care to maintain discipline in their risk control frameworks during periods of prolonged low volatility.

Figure 33: The VIX Reflects the Decline in Volatility

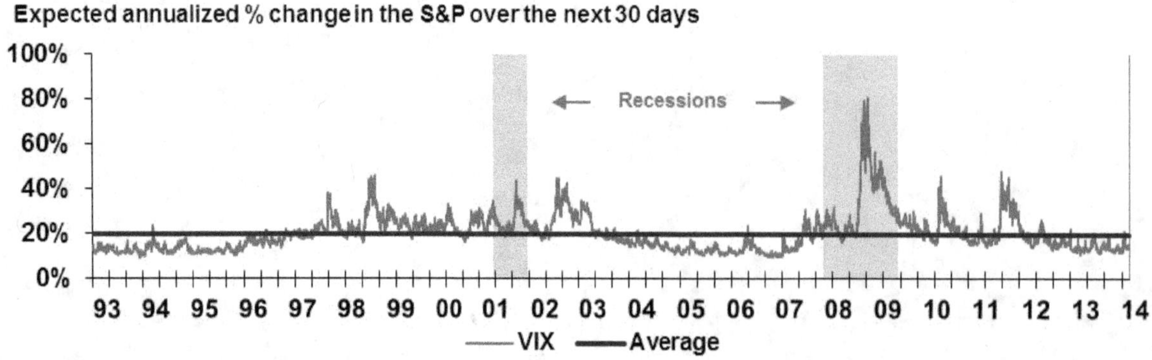

Expected annualized % change in the S&P over the next 30 days

Source: Bloomberg

The Merrill Option Volatility Estimate (MOVE) is a yield curve weighted index of the normalized implied volatility on 1-month Treasury options. It is the weighted average of volatilities on the 2-, 5-, 10-, and 30-year Treasuries. Market participants often refer to the MOVE as the bond market's fear index. A high number reflects fear while a low number reflects complacency. Historically, sustained readings below 80 suggest extreme complacency, encouraging an increase in risk appetite as banks and other market participants view future price changes as more likely to occur within a narrow band. Such periods have often preceded instability in markets. The MOVE touched an all-time low in December 2012 and remained low until the second quarter of 2013 when concerns arose over the potential for reduced monetary policy accommodation (see figure 34). The MOVE has receded from its recent high and dropped well below its long-term average of 100.

Figure 34: The MOVE Index Reflects the Decrease in Bond Volatility

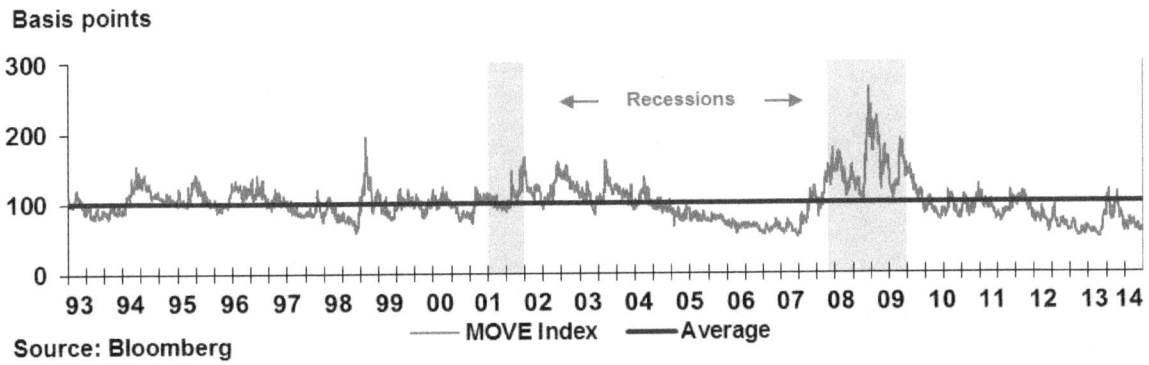

Source: Bloomberg

Home Prices Rising

Generally, rising home prices encourage more aggressive real estate lending. As collateral values rise, reducing stated LTV ratios can lead to significant losses once price growth moderates. The S&P/Case-Shiller composite home price index covering 20 large U.S. metropolitan markets provided some advance warning of the recent housing bubble and subsequent collapse. Figure 35 shows the year-over-year percentage changes in this home price index over time, with growth of about 10 percent during the past two quarters. Although the recent 10 percent annual price increases seem similar to those in 2003 in the early stages of the last home price bubble, it is important to note that in the current climate, all-cash investor sales have played an inordinate role in driving up home prices from their post-bust low points, especially in many of the hardest-hit markets. Thus, the risk to underwriting standards from excessive optimism on real estate prices is likely low now.

Figure 35: Long-Term Trends in the S&P/Case-Shiller 20-City Composite Home Price Index

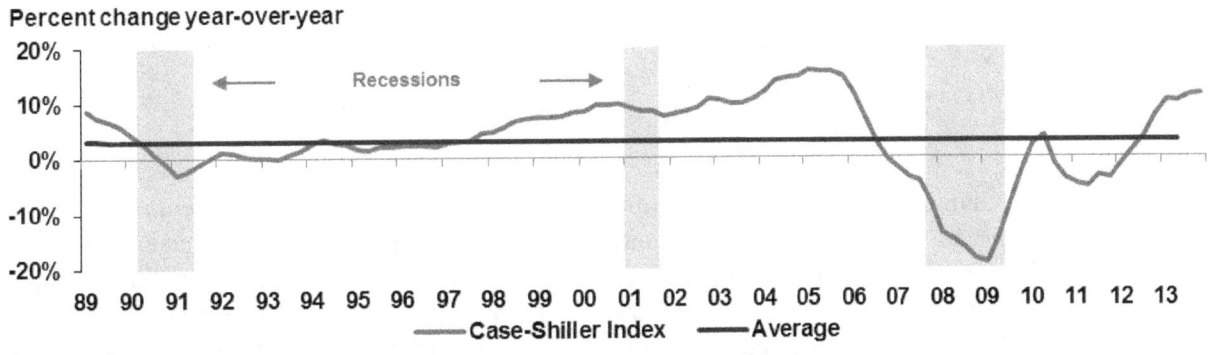

Source: Bloomberg

Part V: Regulatory Actions

Number of Banks Rated 4 or 5 Continues to Decline

The number of OCC-supervised banks rated 4 or 5 continues to decline after peaking in 2011 (see figure 36). The decline is mainly attributable to positive trends in the institutions resulting from the slowly improving economy and recapitalizations.

Figure 36: Number of Banks Rated 4 or 5

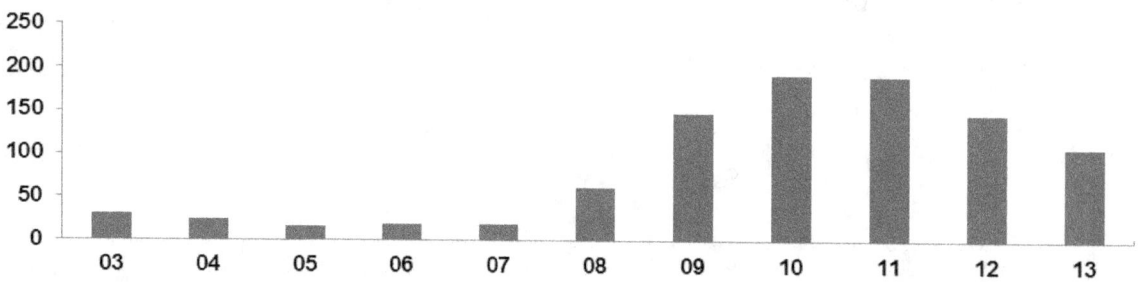

Source: OCC
Note: All data as of year-end.

Matters Requiring Attention Decline

The OCC uses MRAs in the supervisory process when bank practices deviate from safe and sound banking practices or sound risk management principles. Such deviations, if not addressed appropriately, may adversely affect a bank's earnings, capital, risk profile, compliance, or reputation and could lead to formal enforcement action. The number of outstanding MRAs shows a decline through the end of 2013 (see figure 37). The increase in 2012 reflects the addition of 560 federal savings associations that were supervised by the Office of Thrift Supervision prior to the Dodd–Frank Act.

Figure 37: Trend in Outstanding MRAs

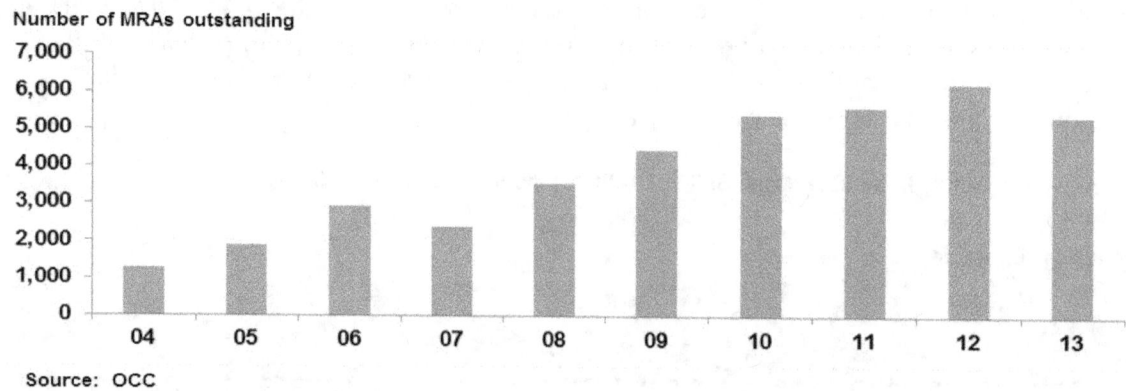

Source: OCC

The top five MRA categories for small banks remain unchanged from the fall 2013 *Semiannual Risk Perspective.* They are credit administration (31 percent), compliance (15 percent), management (11 percent), information technology (9 percent), and audit (6 percent). For large banks, the top five categories also remain unchanged, with MRAs centered in credit risk (29 percent), operational risk (21 percent), BSA/AML (14 percent), consumer compliance (11 percent), and internal controls (10 percent).

Enforcement Actions Against Banks Continue to Decline in 2013

The OCC uses enforcement actions to address more acute problems or weaknesses requiring corrective measures. Informal enforcement actions include commitment letters, memorandums of understanding, and approved safety and soundness plans. Formal enforcement actions, which are disclosed to the public, include cease-and-desist orders, capital directives, and formal agreements. The OCC issued fewer enforcement actions against banks during 2013 than in recent years (see figure 38), reflecting the overall improvement in the condition of federally chartered banks. Nevertheless, some enforcement actions continue to result in significant fines.

Figure 38: Enforcement Actions Against Banks

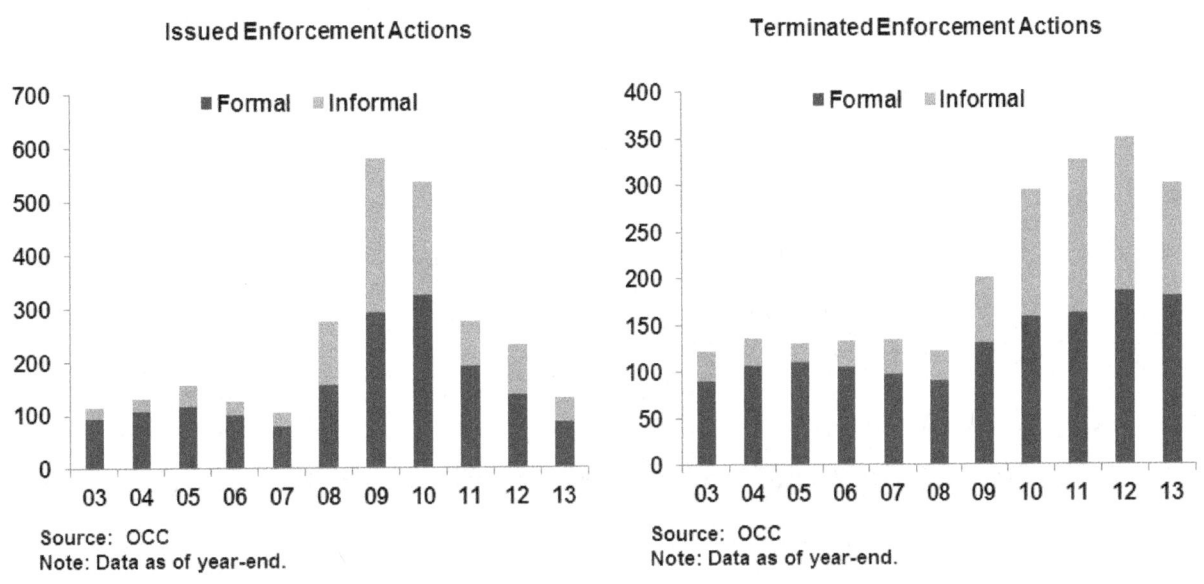

Source: OCC
Note: Data as of year-end.

Index of Figures